WHY YOUR RÉSUMÉ ISN'T WORKING

And How You Can Fix It NOW

Wendy D. Steele

1

Why Your Resume Isn't Working

Career Diamond Books

BluePrint Publishing Group

2451 Cumberland Pkwy. SE Suite 3458

Atlanta, GA 30339

Printed in the United States of America

Career Diamond Books is an imprint of BluePrint Publishing Group,

a division of BluePrint Career Group, LLC

First Printing

Trade Paperback ISBN: 978-1-7327122-3-2

Cover Design by Dave: JD & J Photography

Acknowledgements

As always I have to thank my hubby Craig for being there when I started BluePrint Résumés & Consulting, creating and maintaining our website, helping me with network administration (because you know I've forgotten so much since my IT days) and for continuing to be my sounding board. I'm going in several different directions, but you don't mind. I appreciate you for letting me be me. Of course I continuously thank my sister Tiffany Daniels. If you had not been in need of a resume, well you know that's how it all started. My dear daughter Whitney, to think you are now a Senior Recruiter! Seems like just yesterday you were learning all about HR and assisting our clients. Now I come to you for advice. You are amazing. Once again, my editor Karen Rodgers, thank you for keeping me on my toes. I keep learning so much from you. Natasha Miller, my layout and graphic designer, Dave Roberts at JD&J Photography, thank you for a magnificent cover. Camille Rahatt and Megan Westbrook you were the first two on my editing team. Thank you for completing the manuscript during your hectic schedules.

A Special Thank You

Thank you to all of the executive recruiters and staffing agencies who entrusted me to assist your job candidates and employees. Special thanks goes to Act1 Personnel Services for my first few clients and to Bill Creekmuir of Pinnacle Search for sending me your senior and C-level clients. It has been a joy to work with you for all of these years! I would also like to thank the major Fortune 100 to Fortune 500 companies who called BluePrint Resumes and Consulting first for their outplacement and resume workshop and consulting needs. University professors, I will never forget you. As many shied away from resume writing companies, I am grateful that those of you in Atlanta saw the value in providing that extra help to your students.

And lastly, to our clients, I will be forever grateful that you too chose BluePrint Resumes & Consulting out of the hundreds of other professional resume writing companies in the world. Even international job candidates. How did you ever find us? Amazing! Because of our thankful and loyal clients, we have a huge referral base. We also have a huge repeat client base due to career transitioners, promotions and more. Thank you for always thinking of us for your resume and job search consulting needs. My main goal has always been to make a positive difference in your job search. As I always say, without you there would be no BluePrint Resumes & Consulting.

Client Comments

The following are just a few compliments from some of our happy clients.

Good morning Wendy,

I wanted to thank you for all the hard work, time, and professional insight you put into the resumes, cover letter, as well as my LinkedIn page. One interviewer stated that my resume was the best he had seen in almost 30 years. Another stated how professional my resume looked, and a third said he was very impressed with my resume. That speaks volumes of you and the service you provide. Thank you so much and I truly wish you years of success. Professionally,

Bryan S.

Good Morning Wendy-

Hope all is well with you and your family!

I wanted to let you know that I landed a job with my new resume working for Kennesaw State University in the Cultural and Community Centers. I am so happy to be working with such a great team of people and I have you to thank for that! Thank you again for all your support and guidance and I will forward your name to all my family & friends that are looking to update their resume.
Warm regards,

T. C.

Wendy,

Thanks for sending. In my second phone interview yesterday the regional director said "hey, as a side note, your resume looks phenomenal. When I get ready to update my resume I want to find out who helped you with that." So, great job!

Jennifer

Wendy!

Let me say thank you so very much...in less than a year and a layoff your unique outstanding talent reflected in the task of combining my experience paid off. I was offered a position with a law firm... healthcare law. I thought it was far-fetched but the expertise caught their attention. Thank you...between you and God I'm so blessed. I get to work in a new atmosphere, new role!

Thanks

Angie

Hey Wendy just wanted to give you an update. Since my resume was redone by you I received callbacks from 2 airlines. Kallita air and Air Wisconsin. After 3 rounds of interviews with each company I received offers from both Airline's. Thank you so much for your help.

Sincerely

Jerri B.

FAA Certified Flight Dispatcher

Hi Wendy,

I officially accepted an offer for a financial analyst position with Bluestem Brands. I was asked to apply before I was able to talk to you about edits and made a few small changes myself. They must have loved the resume since they offered me the job! Thank you so much for all your hard work and helping me present myself to potential employers. I will be suggesting Blueprint to all my friends! You rock!

Thank you so much!

Whitney H.

Another comment in addition to a previous one sent:

Hi Wendy!

I hope all is well! Any chance Ginger and I get we always let people know the excellent job you and your staff have done for both of us. And once we show them our resume they want your contact info ASAP. That is a testament to the GREAT work you all do. We are both doing great at the moment, but will definitely be in touch when we need your services. Take care!

Kind Regards,

Tony

To my senior writer and I:

Hi Wendy and Trista,

Just a quick update to let you know that I have obtained a new position! I credit Blueprint Resumes a great deal for helping me get not one, but two offers :). I chose one and began my new job today. I am now a Program Manager with Belk Stores, Inc. (still here in Charlotte).

Thank you so much for the work that you and Trista have put into helping me achieve new things in my career. Now...I still have to let you actually update my LinkedIn Profile - LOL! My apologies, as you can probably guess, I was so busy interviewing that I never got around to actually giving you info to make the updates.

Again, just wanted to give you both a big THANK YOU!

Audrey

Another note regarding our senior writer:

Trista did a great job and it was a pleasure working with her. I have gotten very good feedback on the resume presentations from accounting recruiter.

Thank you both so very much for your help.

Sherry H.

And there are hundreds more. You can also view additional comments and reviews on Google and several other review and referral sites.

Introduction

Imagine… you've just been denied the promotion you so desperately deserve for the third time, in five years! Rob has been promoted as well as Ashley and you know good and well they don't know half of what you know. All they do is take credit for other people's work. All of this coming in at the crack of dawn and staying so late, you might as well keep a sleeping bag under your desk, since you'll be back at it in about four hours anyway…*Enough!* you think out loud. You're tired of giving all of your talent to these leeches. So on your next break you get online and hit the job search engines—the big ones like Indeed, Career Builder and Monster. You view lots of job opportunities in your field. Look at Glassdoor! Employees even tell you what it's like to work for their company. You think, *"While I'm at it, I should write a review for this prison I'm about to get out of."* This is why you've been keeping your resume updated every few years… just in case, because you knew it was coming.

You post your resume to all three, or all four of the job boards. You make sure your cell is on vibrate, so you don't miss a call from the hiring manager (or managers) who are sure to track you down and breathlessly beg you to come in for an interview any day now. And you wait… and wait… and wait. You wonder what's up, so you review your profile again. *Check.* You took the address off your resume because you heard that's a big no. *Check.* Review your resume again to make sure you have your objective, degree, skills and all of your 10-15 years of experience, same as you've always done. *Check, check, check!* Oh, one thing you notice you forgot. The cover letter! That's the problem right there! It said you could add one. How in the world did you forget? So you quickly write one reiterating your expertise, upload that bad boy along with your masterpiece of a resume and you're good to go. And then you wait… and wait… and… wait.

Two months roll by and you've gotten maybe two hits from your resume, but they're nowhere near what you've been applying for. Not only that, but your manager just sent out a blast email about a going away party for your coworker Rob, the one who does nothing really.

He's leaving the company to go on to greener pastures: a higher paying job with some Fortune 100 company. What the ...? Later on you ask Rob, "So how did you find out about this job?" He says, "Oh, I just posted my resume on Indeed, Career Builder, Monster, oh and Glassdoor and started getting calls within a week! It took a while to make up my mind on who to go with and I was tired of going on all of these interviews…." You drown him out of your thoughts as you stare into space. Finally, you decide Rob is just a unicorn!

You're in the break room the next day getting a cup of coffee. A few other coworkers are in there and they're all talking about *Rob,* his new starting salary and everything. You pull your resume up on your phone and ask Christie to take a look at it. She says, "Oh, you don't have nearly enough of your experience listed." Another coworker overhears the two of you and he walks over. "Why's your education, way down here? You need to move that up." Two more people come over and they're experts too. You don't listen to all of them, but Christie used to work in HR, so you know she knows what she's talking about, so you take her advice. One of the others used to be a manager in the department next door, so you know he knows even more than Christie. You thank them, rush back to your desk, polish the resume up again and repost it to all four sites. And then… crickets. "Oh forget it!" you say… "I'll just apply for that promotion again. This is too much work."

So What is a Resume?

Most job candidates today have a general idea of what a resume is, but do not know how to craft one properly or what it should and should not include. Many people who have never needed one assume it's either a simple document listing your employment, skills, and education so that you can get a job, or that it's a long detailed history of your places of employment and so on. At the time of this writing, Merriam-Webster defines a resume as: a short document describing your education, work history, etc., that you give an employer when you are applying for a job, a list of achievements, a short description of things that have happened.

This definition is true; however, people take that at face value not realizing it's a little more than that. No one knows what every hiring manager is looking for these days, but the consensus of opinion is that a resume must do the following three things:

- Get the candidate through the initial scanning process
- Draw enough interest for the reader to at least get half way down the page
- Prompt a job interview

A resume is a marketing tool to help you get job interviews. You are using this tool to market and sell yourself and it needs to describe your overall experience succinctly. Now, getting back to the dictionary's definition. The *short document* part of Webster's definition is subjective since what may be short to one person may not be short to another, and your resume shouldn't be so short as to leave important information out. You do need to give brief details, but they should be specific, and not too long. And yes, a resume should always have achievements. Whatever you put on your resume, you must be able to back up and/or prove during the interview. There are also certain general rules that one must follow which I discuss throughout this book. These are simple things and myths you should avoid, as they can and will determine whether a hiring manager will call you in for an interview or add you to the trash folder.

By the way, the proper way of spelling resume is with the accents like this: résumé, but it's okay now to spell it both ways. For the sake of distraction, I left the accents off in most pages of the book.

Keep in mind as you read this book, that what works for one hiring manager or recruiter may not work for another. There are always exceptions to the rules. Some things you've probably heard of, but wonder if they are true, false, or if things have changed. I have been writing resumes since the mid-90s, first for colleagues and now professionally as a part of the BluePrint Résumés & Consulting group for the last 13 years. Each of the possible reasons for why your resume may not be working, are problems I've seen with our clients throughout the years. Some I figure are a given and I started not to even add them, but I'm still seeing the same things from clients, even today. These are not just entry-level career seekers. No, these are professionals with 5, 10, or more years of experience, and managers with 15 years or more under their belts. Some people have just been out of the game for so long, or never needed a resume for their particular industry, or… just knew someone, who knew someone, who also… knew someone. Back in the day, nepotism was real!

So I figured why not? The guidelines in this book are based on what I have learned, and more specifically what most recruiters and hiring managers look for. Remember, the main thing is to make sure your resume stands out among the rest so that you not only get interviews, but *quality* interviews.

How This Book Is Structured

This book is divided into four sections:

First, I go over the basics that most people already know. I point out all the reasons why your resume isn't working. Next, it gets deeper with the not-so-basic stuff. Things that you, or the person you know who's struggling, may not have ever thought of or noticed about the resume. They of course won't all apply to you, but since you're reading this book you will probably see some reasons that are keeping you from being able to get in front of the right hiring manager and show them the rock star you are, who's been climbing the charts for years. In section two I explain how to handle these shortcomings, which is the subtitle of the book— How You Can Fix It NOW. I actually show you how to overcome the problems in Section one too, but section two goes into those sticky situations that many people run into. I detail how to fix those on the resume.

Section three is all about the delivery. And I mean the *right* way. Section four has some extras for federal government job seekers and how to craft a cover letter. Lastly, I have some goodies for you at the end of the book. ☺ Oh, and I have humorous quotes at the beginning of most chapters. Not all of them because I ran out of quotes. I'm speaking for the hiring manager. After all, I know what most are thinking. I'm one myself. Some of them are reasonable. Others are just ridiculous. We discuss this all the time. Okay I know, on with it already. Here we go!

SECTION I

The Basic and Not So Basic

Chapter 1

First, Let's Get Rid of the Myths

Myth #1: You Must Use an Objective (or you'll die) Or Don't Use One (and you'll surely die)

This is the #1 myth for a reason. Because it's the first thing after your contact information on a resume. Of course, it wasn't always a myth. For years we put the big fat Objective as the heading at the top of a resume because it showed what you were seeking, right? Well, the problem with the Objective is that it tells what you want when you need to show a hiring manager how you can produce what they want. You may (or may not) be aware that we use summaries today. Some people will try using an Objective and a Summary at the top of a resume. That's a definite no because the summary is enough. If you must use an Objective, do so in a different way, by stating your job target at the top and the field or position you're applying for. By all means do not use that old-fashioned Objective that screams, "This is All About Me and I Expect You to Give Me What I Want!" Or just list your current title if you're applying for a related job. Whether you add the title of the position you're targeting or your current one, you still want to make sure you provide a nice lead-in with information that is relevant to the position you're applying for. Make sense? If not, don't worry, I have provided some examples further in the book.

Myth #2: The One-Page Rule, No Exceptions!

Lately, I've been thinking about making this the #1 myth. No matter how many decades go by, it seems that hundreds still believe in the one-page rule. The one-page rule generally applies to new graduates. A new graduate usually will not have much experience in their targeted industry, so the resume is expected to only be one page. An experienced professional would expect to have up to two pages. Some resumes such as IT or a senior-level/director can go to three. A federal resume can even go up to five pages! Two pages is the norm for experienced professionals with say, five or more years of experience and more than one job listed. We always try not to go over two. Remember, it's the content that matters most. I don't care that Elon Musk was able to do a one-page resume. It doesn't apply to everyone or every situation.

Now, having said all that, I know you've probably run into a recruiter, hiring manager, friend who's a hiring manager or some other person, who is adamant about you squeezing 10-20 years of your work experience onto one page no matter what. So for those people who are just too impatient, have way too many resumes to review with no help, or whatever the reason is, I offer this advice. If your resume is over a page and you're worried, keep two versions handy: a one-page and a two-page (or page and a half if you don't quite fill up the second page). We've done that for our executive clients before and still made their resume pack a punch.

Myth #3: You need to add community service or volunteer experience.

Years ago you added these things (and even hobbies!) because it showed what a well-rounded person you were. These days unless it's relevant to the job posting, it's not necessary to add them. It would be appropriate if you're a new college graduate and you were very active in various extra-curricular activities while maintaining a 3.5 – 4.0 GPA. In that case it could even be a plus for you. Also for the more experienced candidate, I'm not saying not to add community service or volunteer experience at all, I'm saying add them if they meet one of the following:

> ➢ They're relevant to the job posting (as previously mentioned).
> ➢ They're current.
> ➢ There aren't too many. This could make the hiring manager wonder if you have time for the job you're applying for.
> ➢ You have enough room on the resume to add them. They can make nice space fillers.

Bottom line, if they add nothing to the resume, leave them off!

Myth #4: You should use different fonts and make your name as large as you can to make the resume stand out more.

I see this quite often, mainly with some international resumes. There are some domestic novices as well. If you make your name too large, it overshadows the rest of the resume. This, along with too many different fonts, can make the resume appear too busy and distracting. There is a way to liven up a resume and make it pop without all of the unnecessary fluff.

Myth #5: References Upon Request is a must!

This rule went out a few years ago. It is assumed that you will provide references if a hiring manager requests them. Why would you not? So it's not necessary to add that at the bottom of a resume. That's another example of just filling space. And by all means please do not add your references to the resume or even submit a separate sheet of references until you are requested to do so.

Myth #6: You should add all of your skills and entire work history. They could come in handy!

No, you should not. Only include what's relevant to the job or industry you're targeting. Further along in this book you will see an example of a resume that touches on this very myth. You want the hiring manager or recruiter to see what direction you're going in. If you add auditing, truck driving, real estate, and a number of other non-related skills for an accounting job, whomever is reading your resume may become quite confused. Of course those skills are exaggerated, but you get the idea, right?

Myth #7: Never use color or graphs, they're too fancy.

This used to be a huge no years ago. Reason being was one, they were too distracting, and two, most resumes were printed, taken in person, or mailed. Different colors would not show up well on resumes, so the rule of thumb was just to always use black. Today's resumes, however, are usually emailed or posted to job boards, so it's okay to use color, but sparingly. By sparingly I mean around a border or maybe a title and in neutral, dark colors like blue. Even a dark red is fine, depending on the industry. As for graphs, it also depends on the industry. Graphs can show a great bit of detail for a sales professional or graphics designer, especially if a sales professional has year-over-year sales increases for the past 10 years. A graph could draw the readers' eyes directly to those numbers, making their job that much easier and encourage them to read further.

Now, I have also heard people say any graphs or gray shading won't show up well when posting your resume to a job search engine. True, which is why you should always have a separate format for those systems. I go into great detail about this as well later in the book.

Myth #8: Always use Spell Check because it catches everything.

No, it doesn't. I'm not saying not to use Spell Check because I am very thankful for it, but I am saying it does not catch everything. Most will use Microsoft Word for this and Word does not recognize fragmented sentences; which, by the way is how resumes are supposed to be written. There are also many words that this tool may not catch because it doesn't know the context you're using them in. I've seen Word mistake an English word for the British way of writing it. For example, maybe you meant to write the word "behavior," and Word corrects it to say "behaviour." And vice versa if you're writing an international resume. Of course making sure you have your grammar and punctuation settings to American English (or UK English) should cure this, but every now and then, Word can miss it.

Another thing I've seen Word do plenty of times is miss a misspelled word that's simply missing a letter. Grammarly is not foolproof either. So sorry, neither one catches everything, and you'd better use a dictionary, The Gregg Reference Manual (it gives you all kinds of rules for business documents), know how to spell, or have your resume proofread by someone before sending it out.

Myth #9: If you went to college, but didn't earn the degree, don't add the school.

What if you only had five more credits to go? Do you want to negate all of that hard work? Furthermore, do you want someone to think that you only went to high school when that's not true? Well, if you leave it off that's exactly what may come to mind. Adding the college shows that you at least attempted to go on to higher education and further your career. All you have to do is list the school, the major, and the degree you worked towards, or simply the school and the major. You can add the years if they were recent or leave them off. The point is to show what I just said above.

Myth #10: You should use a P.O. Box (for any number of reasons). Don't show your address on your resume (because hiring managers discriminate). Or worse, someone could know where you live, come to your house and…

Okay I'm kidding about the last part… kind of, then again there is Google Maps.
No! No! No! Please don't do this! It tells the employer three things: #1, you're not stable, #2, you're hiding something, #3, you probably live too far from the job, which again says you're hiding something.

If you're worried about them finding out where you live, would you rather get the interview, go through the interview, fill out the application, then they find out where you live and you end up not getting the job? I certainly wouldn't want to go through all of that when they'll find out anyway. I go into this a little further later on in the book and give tips on how to handle this. For example, I agree with not including your address when you post your resume online. You can always select the anonymous feature on various job search engines.

Another exception to not adding your address is when you're in transition, such as moving from one city to another. See if you can use a relative or friend's address. Some people work in different states, so their address constantly changes. So again, there are exceptions to everything, but I'm telling you, just omitting it because you don't want an employer to know how far away you live from the company? It can backfire on you. Worried about someone spying on your property through Google Maps? Well, with the hundreds of resumes that recruiters have to sift through and even when narrowed down, I doubt they'll go through the trouble of pulling up every candidate's home on Google Maps. Besides that, it doesn't always show your house, but a street view. Remember, there are tips on how to handle these situations as you read further. Actually, in Chapter 10 titled "Red Flags" if you want to skip on over to it now.

Do You Need a Resume or Curriculum Vitae?

Most job candidates in the U.S. just need a resume to either get started in their career search or to move up within their organization. Some need a Curriculum Vitae, most commonly referred to as a CV. Professors, scientists, researchers, educators with Ph.Ds. and many others who have several publications and lectures under their belts usually need a CV. The only real difference is the CV is lengthier and a little more detailed than your average one-to two-page resume. CVs tend to be an average of three to four pages, depending on the person's background and what recruiters in their field are seeking. Our international clients need CVs, which include most everything I just listed, along with personal information, and in most cases, a photo. If you're a U.S. candidate adding your photo to your resume, please stop! Unless you're a member of the clergy or in a specific industry that requests this, such as film (acting) or broadcasting where you may be a news anchor.

For the U.S. job candidate, the format for a CV starts off pretty similar to a resume. You would start with your introduction (summary or profile) and keywords (which I'll detail) and then go into your experience and education. Once you add your education, the additional information such as publications, seminars, lectures, and inventions would be added. For educational CVs you would need to practically list your entire work history from student teaching all the way to your current job.

In any case, you will know whether you need a resume or CV because the recruiter, hiring manager or the job posting itself will tell you.

Chapter 2

First Problem

You Wait Until the Last Minute

"Just send over your resume. When? Today! The posting comes down in two days!"

Have you ever done this? You're all comfy in your cushiony, well-paying job, steadily moving up the ranks. Or maybe you're complacent, satisfied with just being…satisfied. Maybe you've been on the job for five, ten or fifteen years. You're not going anywhere. This is a great company! Think you don't need a resume? Think again! You may not need one now, but at some point in time you will. It may not be for another five, ten or fifteen years even, but the time to create or update your resume is not when things go bad, when you see the writing on the wall, or hear through the company grapevine that a merger or acquisition is about to happen. The time is now.

Why? Well, most would say it's because you never know what will happen. Tomorrow is not promised to anyone; you can't trust these jobs; job security is gone and so on. All of these are obvious; however, another crucial reason to make sure you don't wait is because…

Drum roll please… You rush! That's right. That little quote at the top is really from several recruiters and job candidates who call us all the time telling us a recruiter or friend told them those exact words. The recruiters are trying to fill quotas and complete contracts.

Here's what happens when you rush:

You just throw something together. Anything that looks decent because you're trying to meet a tight deadline. You end up leaving out all kinds of pertinent information that would sell you because you're in a hurry and don't take the time to think of a strategy for applying to the job you're targeting. I'll explain in a little bit, and you'll see what all of that pertinent information is.

If you don't write it yourself (because of course you're in a hurry and don't have time with work and all), you start asking friends and coworkers. No luck there, and they're just wasting your time. So you start calling around to professional resume writing companies. You've just heard about these companies, or maybe you did years ago, but never needed to use one because, well you never needed a resume. And when you did, back then you were perfectly capable of creating your own. After all, it's how you got this job! Now you know nothing about these resume writing companies and as you're searching Google, you find there are about 600 or so of them out there! They run anywhere from $10 a page, hmm… don't want that, to $500-$1000 a pop! Definitely can't afford that. You say, "Good gracious, do I even need a professionally written resume?" You need something affordable, efficient and fast! You don't have time to do exhaustive research, so you go with the first company that can provide this.

They're in just as much of a hurry to take your money as you are to make the money you so deserve so *BAM*… Here's your resume. Good-bye. It's not that good. Or maybe it is… to *you*. You send it off to the recruiter, who (and you don't know this), by now has a sea of qualified candidates ahead of you. Your result? Nothing.

And what about when your dream job or opportunity comes up internally? This happened to me once. It's actually how I started writing resumes for my coworkers. One day, our IT trainer came to us and said that our new manager told her to go to a select group of people and get their resume. Apparently, it was discovered that the pay rate had recently changed for our market and we weren't being compensated fairly. Other Fortune 500 companies similar to ours, were paying their employees more than what we were making for doing the same job! So the powers that be figured they'd better get up to par, or risk a lawsuit. Yaay! We're about to get *paid,* right? Not so fast. There were stipulations. In order to get the increase, not only were we to submit the resume by a deadline, like… in two days, but we had to show on that resume why we not only deserved the increase, the actual pay we were supposed to get that they had been denying us for who knows how long, but we also needed to show that we even deserved our *current* salary. And if we didn't we would be axed! That's right. Out the door quick!

Needless to say, I rushed. Talk about sweating bullets! I hadn't written a resume in eons, but I knew how to write one. Well, so I thought. I quickly pulled one from several years ago, updated that baby with my current job and voilà! I sent it to my new manager. And… he sent it back. I was crushed. All hope was not lost though. I knew he was shaking his head at me in shame, but he politely told me, "Just check Microsoft Word for some ideas." Ideas on what? Template designs were all I could think of. Then he briefly explained what he needed to see. He couldn't tell me how to actually rewrite the resume, but he could point me to the tools and resources I needed for a quick tutorial.

So I did what he said. I rewrote my resume, turned into Captain Save-an-Employee and you know what? I not only got to keep my job, my usual 5% pay raise (my performance review was coming up), but I got a 13% increase! I was so ecstatic! From then on, I was doing everybody's resume.

Okay, so my situation turned into a happy ending, but many don't. This is why people say to update your resume every six months. I say update it every time you take on a new task, have an achievement, fill in for somebody on maternity leave, complete a project and so on. At least keep a running tally of things. This way when you do need a resume, you're not the one rushing at the last minute unprepared, get rejected and don't get the interview.

Chapter 3

You Don't Have a Job Target

*"We do NOT want a renaissance hero! And I don't care if you do have transferable skills for the 10 other positions in our company. I just need you to fit **this** posting."*

Most of our clients do have a specific target, but the information on their resume is non-relevant, or doesn't contain enough examples to show them as a leader in their field. A common problem we see, especially when there's a tight job market, is someone who is a jack-of-all-trades. Maybe you're a master at some and right now you just want to find a job in any one of your desired fields just so that you can earn a decent living. For example, you recently switched careers to Human Resources, but until a good generalist or management position comes along you figure you'll also apply for something in sales, elementary education, or even customer service since you see tons of job openings in customer service every day.

So you decide to put your human resources, sales, school teaching (from when you taught fourth grade social studies for five years) and customer service experience all on one resume. You've listed everything you can think of that will show how you are a highly qualified candidate for any one of those fields. Now you submit that fabulous resume to any and every job posting that says: Human Resource Generalist, Sales Representative, Fourth Grade Social Studies Teacher, Call Center Customer Service Representative, and so on...

This is what we call a one-size-fits-all resume. And they usually don't work. Today's resumes have to be targeted to one field. If yours is targeted to the job you are applying for as much as possible that's even better! Does this mean that you have to have a different resume for each field? If the fields you're interested in are completely different, then I'm afraid the answer is a resounding yes.

So How Do I Do This?

The best way to handle this is to narrow down your choices to what you really want to do, and if any of your fields of expertise are related, then you can put those on the same resume. This will cut down on the number of different versions you'll need. See the examples on the next page.

First, let's start with two new graduate examples because a lot of new graduates do the basic resume where you just add your education at the top and then the experience, as if the education alone should suffice. Sometimes it does, and again it depends on the hiring manager and the company. You still should make yourself stand out. Notice these new graduate resumes are geared towards the major and the job target. For the first one, since the candidate only had three years of work experience, we elaborated on the candidate's projects.

The second example shows a candidate with courses to supplement the small amount of actual work experience he had.

COREY BELCHER

12631 Keyworth Dr. | Houston, TX 77014 | 832-336-1021 |coreyb@gmail.com

VALUE OFFERED TO YOUR ORGANIZATION

Dependable, action-oriented new graduate with an impressive history of supply chain related courses and projects. Described as a valued team member offering solid customer service and interpersonal skills. Detail-oriented, consistently maintaining a near zero error rate in demanding conditions. Bilingual in English and Spanish.

CORE COMPETENCIES

Planning | Purchase Orders | Cost of Goods Sold (COGS) | Scheduling | Organization
Inventory & Materials Management | Vendor Management | Problem Solving
Software: Microsoft Word, Excel, PowerPoint, Publisher, Access | SAP

EDUCATION

UNIVERSITY OF HOUSTON – C.T. BAUER COLLEGE OF BUSINESS | TX
Bachelor of Business Administration in Supply Chain Management | May 2018
Honors: Magna Cum Laude; Dean's List Spring 2017 and Fall 2016

SUPPLY CHAIN MANAGEMENT PROJECTS

FMC Technologies Strategic Sourcing Competition Champion | Fall 2017
- Analyzed annual spend data for procurement of mission critical parts for Enhanced Vertical Deepwater Trees.
- Conceived a sourcing strategy focused on building vendor relationships in the region.
- Produced potential hard and soft cost savings forecast to exceed $4.3 million.

SAP Competitive Simulation Champion | Fall 2016
- Managed cash-to-cash cycle time using Enterprise Resource Planning software (SAP).
- Cut cash conversion cycle (CCC) by 60% from 94 to 38 days by 4th quarter.
- Evaluated data from SAP and used Crystal Dashboard to create reports.

PROFESSIONAL EXPERIENCE

SPLASH WATERPARK | Spring, TX   **Area Supervisor**   May 2015 – Dec. 2018

Monitored $2 million food service inventory with over 150 products. Managed and scheduled 30-40 employees; tracked labor hours to ensure adequate staff and smooth flow of operations.
- Collaborated in the development of a customized weekly inventory management system on Excel that calculated and documented damages, losses and Cost of Goods Sold (COGS).
- Drove significant sales increase for every stand while reducing COGS by 3% from 2012 to 2013.

ORGANIZATIONS

INSTITUTE FOR SUPPLY MANAGEMENT | **Member**   Spring 2016 – Present
HISPANIC BUSINESS STUDENTS ASSOCIATION | **Member**   Fall 2015 – Present

ANTONIO BAKER

223 Candy Ct. SW • Atlanta, Georgia 30314• Cell: (404) 324-4626 • antonbaker@cau.edu

SUMMARY OF QUALIFICATIONS

College senior possessing sound analytical and math skills suitable for financial analyst or financial services position. Knowledge of U.S. and foreign stock markets with **additional competencies in:**
Microsoft Word, Excel and PowerPoint…Cash Flow Analysis…Forecasting…Market Theory
Stock and Bond Valuation…Global Trading…Derivatives…Financial and Income Statements

EDUCATION

Clark Atlanta University, Atlanta, GA   December 2018
Bachelor of Business Administration: Concentration in Finance
GPA: 3.5, Honors Program

Related Courses
□ Personal Finance/Corporate Finance   □ Commercial Bank Management
□ Financial Markets and Institutions   □ International Financial Management
□ Security Analysis and Portfolio Management   □ Retirement Planning/Employee Benefits

Academic Project
Financial Management Class: Developed a mock client portfolio with various investments for a moderate risk taker. Portfolio produced the highest rate of return (10%) among 12 other students' portfolios. Received A+ grade.

EMPLOYMENT EXPERIENCE

NEW YORK STOCK EXCHANGE (NYSE), New York, NY   May 2018- Dec. 2018
Floor Operations Intern
- Performed various tasks on the trading floor while learning new technologies.
- Set up trading halts and ensured all market makers properly opened and closed their stocks.
- Attended multiple meetings involving migration of broker systems, in the absence of supervisor.
- Joined other interns in listening to lecturers from financial professionals at top companies such as Goldman Sachs and Credit Suisse.
- Developed a 100-page PowerPoint presentation on improvements in the trading process.
- Learned numerous computer systems used on the floor in a very short time span.

VOLUNTEER EXPERIENCE

MUST Ministries Thanksgiving and Christmas Food Drive   2016 – 2018

ORGANIZATIONS
Business Leaders Initiative (BLI), Member, 2014-Present
Omega Psi Phi Fraternity, Inc., Treasurer, 2012-Present

Experienced Professional Example #1

JESSICA ADAMS

1654 Spring Drive ▪ Baltimore, MD 21212
410.427.6234 (H) ▪ 202.258.3222 (C) ▪ jadams123@gmail.com

HUMAN RESOURCES PROFESSIONAL

Result-driven professional with over 10 years of combined experience in customer service and human resources. Able to work independently as well as part of a team, while utilizing excellent decision making skills. Delivered high quality of service in all roles and recognized as a leader who gets results.

CORE COMPETENCIES

Relationship Building | Customer Service | Conflict Resolution & Problem Solving
Employee Relations | Employee Training | Recruitment | Employment Laws
Benefits | Administrative Support /Job Fairs Support | New Hire Orientation

PROFESSIONAL EXPERIENCE

CALDWELL, BLACK & WEST, Baltimore, MD   2011 – Present
Human Resources Generalist
Perform HR administrative support and recruiting duties for a law firm of 200 attorneys. Assist with job fairs at Ivey League universities, telephone screenings for interviews, new hire orientation and manage attorneys' calendars,

► Piloted strategic recruitment effort that reduced 20 associate attorney vacancies
  by 50% within five months of taking on new role.
► Proved instrumental in facilitating job placement opportunities for 10 candidates.
► Significantly improved efficiency of department and services performed through
  continuous effort that included making recommendations on new approaches,
  policies and procedures.

CASE CUSTOMER SOLUTIONS, Towson, MD   2002 – 2011
Customer Service Representative
Worked in a call center environment handling customer service calls for Sprint and Verizon Wireless cellular customers. Assigned to a team of 20 members.
► Successfully met all monthly and quarterly metric goals for call handling time.
► Received five service awards for excellence with internal/external customers.
► Built solid rapport across global division and effectively worked with cross-
  functional teams.

EDUCATION

UNIVERSITY OF MARYLAND, BALTIMORE, MD
Bachelor of Science in Business Administration, 2012

CERTIFICATIONS

Human Resources Management

COMPUTER PROFICIENCY

Microsoft Word, Excel, PowerPoint, Outlook, Lexis-Nexis

Using the example of human resources, sales, elementary education and customer service, there are at least two or three related skill sets and experience that can be used on the same resume. Human resources and customer service for one, because no matter what the role is, you'll need customer service skills, as even the employees can be internal customers. If you're applying for a recruiter position then you may be dealing with external clients.

Example #2

JESSICA ADAMS

1654 Spring Dr. ▪ Baltimore, MD 21212 ▪ 202.258.3222 ▪ jadams@gmail.com

HUMAN RESOURCES SALES & RECRUITMENT

Result-driven professional with over 10 years of combined experience in customer service, sales and human resources. Able to work independently as well as part of a team, while utilizing excellent decision making skills. Delivered high quality of service in all roles and recognized as a leader who gets results.

CORE COMPETENCIES

Relationship Building | Customer Retention | Account Management | B2B Sales
Contract Negotiations | Pre-Screening & Recruitment | Employment Laws
Benefits | Administrative/Job Fairs Support | New Hire Orientation

PROFESSIONAL EXPERIENCE

CALDWELL, BLACK & WEST, Baltimore, MD   2011 – Present
Human Resources Generalist
Perform HR administrative support and recruiting duties for law firm of 200 attorneys. Assist with job fairs at Ivey League universities, telephone screenings for interviews, new hire orientation and manage attorneys' calendars for interviews.

- ► Piloted strategic recruitment effort that reduced 20 associate attorney vacancies by 50% within five months of taking on new role.
- ► Proved instrumental in facilitating job placement opportunities for 10 candidates.

Continued on Next Page

PROFESSIONAL EXPERIENCE

CASE CUSTOMER SOLUTIONS Towson, MD   2002 – 2011
Sales Account Manager/ Customer Care Representative: 2005 – 2011
Managed 10 major accounts consisting of various telecommunications companies. Sourced and recruited candidates for different positions. Solicited recruiting services to new and growing firms.

► Secured an average of two new accounts every month for three straight years.
► Implemented new processes and procedures for maintaining clients during the recession.
► Developed and introduced new service offerings including new benefit programs for clients.

Customer Care Representative: 2002 – 2005
Handled customer service calls for Sprint/Nextel and Verizon Wireless cellular customers.

► Successfully met all monthly and quarterly call metric goals for call handling time.
► Received several service awards for excellence with internal/external customers.

EDUCATION

UNIVERSITY OF MARYLAND, BALTIMORE, MD

BS in Business Administration; Certificate in HR Management, 2009

In example #2, we added the additional role the candidate had in sales. Human resources and sales skills could tie in together in case you decided to apply for a third-party recruiting position. Things like negotiation skills, persuasion skills and so on could be useful for an account management position where you'd be responsible for acquiring and maintaining corporate accounts. Notice the elementary education experience really has no relevance, so it is not included in either example. So this would have to be on the separate resume.

Chapter 4

You Don't Meet the Qualifications for the Job Posting

"I don't care if you are a quick learner. I said must have."

How does that saying go, if I had a dollar for every time…? Well, if I had just fifty cents for every time I have had to tell a client, "Make sure you meet the qualifications of a job posting," I would be a billionaire! Out of the thousands of clients we have, which is a huge mix of executives, professionals and new graduates, quite often we'll have a candidate come to us to have their resume prepared for a position they are not suitable for. One might visit us with their targeted position in mind that they are definitely qualified for, but for whatever reason, once their beautifully crafted resume is complete, not only do they apply for jobs the resume was originally targeted for, but they'll turn into non-qualifiers by also applying for any and everything they think they are qualified to do; although they have no experience or proof of experience in that particular skill area.

If a job posting says that you must have a master's degree in X, Y, Z… then by all means you better have it. Do you know that many hiring managers will skip to your education section first to see if you have this? If you don't, they won't even finish reviewing the rest of the resume. If the posting says five years of hands-on experience coordinating and participating in tradeshow events, although you may have experience in planning events for the entire office, this is not the same as coordinating and participating in tradeshow events. You may be an excellent planner and very capable of planning a tradeshow and even manning the booth all day long, but if you do not meet exactly what that posting says and you can't show examples or transferable skills and how they correlate to the posting, then it's best that you don't apply. At least don't expect to be the top candidate and then wonder why no one called you for an interview.

Now, that's not to say that this is set in stone, or people who haven't had the specific experience listed don't get hired because many of them do, but it's usually when the hiring manager knows the person or they are exhausted with trying to find a suitable candidate. This is when as long as the candidate meets some of the qualifications they're given a chance. Don't hold your breath on that though, which is what a lot of candidates do. This is more the exception, not the rule. Oh and trust me, you might be just a temporary seat filler.

As a hiring manager myself I'll give you another example. An employment posting that I create for resume writers starts off by listing the title, location, pay rate, hours and days of the week needed. Then it may continue to read something like this:

Certified Professional Resume Writer

BluePrint Résumés & Consulting, a top national professional resume writing firm headquartered in Atlanta, GA is seeking a Certified Professional Resume Writer for our Mid-Level Executive clients. This is not a subcontracting opportunity, but an hourly, Monday through Friday position.

Minimum Qualifications:

1. Hold a **CPRW** or other certified resume writing credential
2. Have at least two years of professional resume writing experience
3. Have at least three years of Microsoft Word and Windows PC experience
4. Strong editing and proofreading skills
5. Strong customer service skills
6. Effective written and verbal communication skills
7. Associates or bachelor's degree in English, Communications, Journalism, Administrative Assistant or Business Administration/Business Management with a concentration in Human Resources. If no degree, some college is acceptable.

Preferred Qualifications:

1. Experience in building LinkedIn profiles

2.   Experience in human resources, for example: generalist, administrative or another role where you have screened, evaluated or modified resumes on a regular basis

3.   Experience in assisting executives and management level clients

If interested please submit your most recent resume, along with a cover letter and two resume samples with matching cover letters of your best work to: **hr@blueprintresumes.com**

Now the last time I had a posting out like this we had about 100 people apply within the week and not one of them held a CPRW or any other certified resume writer credential. Not only that, but none of the applicants even had professional resume writing experience. Some had never written a resume before in their lives, or held previous roles where they even did editing and proofreading on a regular basis. There was a mix of former marketing and sales professionals, engineers, master's degree holders and candidates from all other kinds of non-related industries and degrees.

We even had a Ph.D. applicant! Again, from a non-related industry. The posting says associates or bachelor's degree or some college. I certainly would not have accepted anything above that for fear of the new hire not staying with us. And I certainly would not accept anyone who wasn't certified, since this involves a very rigorous exam and you must meet standard rules. People have the misconception that because they have good command of the English language, and can probably communicate effectively that those are the only necessary skills needed to write resumes. Or they do not understand what a resume really is or what writing one entails. Now I'm speaking from a professional standpoint and writing resumes as a business. If you are a strong writer, proofreader, or editor, then it doesn't take long to learn how to write a decent, professional-looking resume. One can be trained in a matter of months, but I was not looking for a novice to our field to train. As the posting says, you must be experienced because what takes years is learning to write various kinds of resumes, the consultation or intake process and being able to guide a client in the right direction.

The other error that many candidates make when not paying attention to the job posting is the submission details. If it says to submit a cover letter, then do so. Many times a posting may list what to detail in the cover letter. I remember candidates emailing us with salary requirements, which is a big no! First, I already had the salary listed and second, this practice is just rude. Especially if the posting didn't say to list it in the cover letter. Also most postings will require that you submit all of your documents by email, as my posting example does, or through one of the job search engines if the company posted the job in this manner.

I cannot tell you how many people tried using the back door method (because they knew someone who knew someone at the company), called us with questions that would be answered if they were interviewed, or as one person did, showed up randomly to our office! Some people see this as taking initiative, but the hiring manager who has hundreds of resumes to view, is busy running operations, barely has time to even interview, and only takes people by appointment, sees this as annoying. It could also appear that you don't pay attention or follow directions very well. Not following the job posting can eliminate you from the candidate pool faster than you can hit the submit button.

Chapter 5

Not Using the Right Keywords

"Uh… what do these skills have to do with this job?"

You've probably heard use keywords in your resume over and over again, but what's more important is using related keywords. Some job candidates assume keywords are just your skillset, but the keywords are those specific qualifiers found in the job posting or your targeted industry. These can be your soft skills, such as communication skills, and your hard skills, also known as core competencies, such as public speaking or contract management. A software developer may have keywords related to his or her specific area like Java or C++, which are the hard technical skills, and the not-so-technical skills, such as meeting project deliverables and deadlines or understanding design implementation. Some soft skills might be working with cross-functional teams or communicating with non-technical end-users. An administrative assistant might have keywords such as: Microsoft Office, particularly Excel and PowerPoint, calendar management or meeting planning, and the soft skills of attention to detail, being able to multitask, prioritizing and meeting deadlines.

Not only is it important to use the right keywords to show that you meet the requirements of the posting, but if you don't use them, most scanning systems will not pick up your resume.

The scanning system I'm referring to is called an Applicant Tracking System (or ATS) and most companies use it now to wade through the thousands of resumes submitted. Many are designed to automatically eliminate you if your resume doesn't show that you meet the minimum qualifications. Whether you are applying externally or internally, this is usually the first step your resume goes through before an actual human reviews it. Soon Artificial

Intelligence (AI) systems will become more prevalent than ATS systems. These are resume-parsing engines. You'll find more on ATS systems later in this book.

Suppose you see some vague postings. You know, the kind that tell you all of the good things you want to hear, such as the pay rate, full-time, the perfect title, your roles and responsibilities and so on, only they leave out another important factor… the qualifications. They may have the education requirements, but you have no idea how many years of experience they want you to have or what industry they want you to have it in. Well, you can do a few things. One, you can show how you're able to meet those roles and responsibilities. For example, if the posting is for an account manager and it says that you must manage national accounts.

National Accounts is a keyword. You could even say *experience in handling national accounts*. If the posting is extremely vague (a lot of job postings in the film industry are this way), you can find keywords all over the internet by doing a keyword search, or pulling up similar job postings from other companies. Now keep in mind, one company may prefer one skill over another, but you can find one that is a very close match. Lastly, keywords are usually at the bottom of certain job search engine pages.

Of course there are those occasions where some systems will pick your resume for positions that you know you don't have keywords on your resume for, or at least you don't think you do. Those are those pesky scam postings or commission only sales job postings. The ones where I advise you to make your contact info (remember the address?) anonymous. You're thinking, Hey, I'm an elementary math teacher. I know I didn't apply for sales, nor do I have the faintest idea of how to sell anything, yet I keep getting all of these jobs sent to my inbox. Well, there are those unscrupulous companies where any word will pass the keyword test. They are just looking for any and every human being they can find. Just ignore those. The best ways to minimize these are:

⇒ Add as many keywords in your resume as you can that are related to the positions you're targeting.

⇒ Use a separate email address just for your job search. This way you don't have to worry about non-essential emails cluttering up your inbox.

⇒ Post your resume to company websites when given the opportunity and post to industry related job search sites such as healthcareers.com or another site for your industry.

And if you start receiving crazy telephone calls, then you may want to select the anonymous button when posting your resume where only your city, state and email address will show. Or if you want to add a phone number, try Google Voice instead.

Regardless of how many bad apples you get, it's still very important to use keywords in your resume. The *right* keywords. The next page shows examples of keywords for today's popular industries and job titles. You'll notice these are actual job postings.

Administrative Assistant at Hire Dynamics
Atlanta, GA 30336

About the Job

MUST HAVE QUICKBOOKS EXPERIENCE, WILL NOT HIRE WITHOUT IT!!!

THIS IS A REQUIREMENT AND RESUME WILL NOT BE READ WITHOUT SEEING SOME EXPERIENCE USING QUICKBOOKS.

- Must have QuickBooks experience
- Office position
- Data entry Experience
- Ordering freight
- Sending monthly invoices to customers
- Printing labels, etc.
- Detail oriented
- May be asked to pick orders
- Forklift preferable
- Confirming Shipments
- Customer service experience
- - Fri. 8am-5pm (1-hour lunch)

Job Type: Full-time

Job Type: Full-time

Salary: $14.00 to $16.00 /hour

Job summary

Location
Atlanta, GA 30336

Job type
Full Time, Employee

Salary
14.00 - 16.00 $ /year

5/3/2018, 6:27 PM

Working hours: 8 AM - 5 PM

Skills:
- General knowledge of PowerPoint - work with templates
- Strong Excel; exporting, formatting, beautifying
- Formulas and pivot tables are a plus
- 3 years of admin experience
- Outlook

Qualifications:
Please send resumes to
kyle.hemphill@randstadusa.com

Randstad is a world leader in matching great people with great companies. Our experienced agents will listen carefully to your employment needs and then work diligently to match your skills and qualifications to the right job and company. Whether you're looking for temporary, temporary-to-permanent or permanent opportunities, no one works harder for you than Randstad. EEO Employer: Race, Religion, Color, National Origin, Citizenship, Sex, Sexual Orientation, Gender Identity, Age, Disability, Ancestry, Veteran Status, Genetic Information, Service in the Uniformed Services or any other classification protected by law.

Why Your Resume Isn't Working

The first set of bullet points show keywords. The keywords are starred as well.

Administrative Assistant Intermediate level

location: Atlanta, GA   type: Temporary   easy apply   ∨
salary: $19 - $20 per hour

job details:

location: Atlanta, GA

salary: $19 - $20 per hour

date posted: Thursday, May 3, 2018

experience: Experienced

job type: Temporary

industry: Finance and Insurance

reference: S_640403

questions: kyle.hemphill@randstadusa.com

job description

Randstad is seeking experienced administrative assistants for a short term opportunity for a major bank in Atlanta!

Duration: 6-8 weeks temp only - medical leave
Pay: $19-20/hr
Hours: Mon-Friday 8am-5pm
Parking: Street parking
Location: 17th St Nw Atlanta GA United States 30363

Responsibilities:
- ✗ Supporting 5 leaders
- ✗ Responsible for handling calendaring
- ✗ Handle expense reports and travel booking through
- ✗ Concur

Not Using the Right Keywords

Again, I put stars by the key words such as calendaring and Concur.

Certified Medical Assistant

3.1 Women's Care Florida – Lakeland, FL

Apply I

Job   Company   Reviews

Company Rating	Glassdoor Estimated Salar‍
3.1	$13/hour $12

Women's Care Florida has earned a reputation for quality women's healthcare in West Central Florida. We pride ourselves on bei
women's healthcare by employing dedicated and caring individuals that promote our philosophy and success of Exceptional Wom
Patient, Every Time.

We have 65 locations throughout Hillsborough, Pinellas, Pasco, Polk, Lake, Seminole, and Orange counties with plans for future gr
seeking a Certified Medical Assistant to join our dynamic team at our Lakeland OBGYN office in Lakeland, FL.

JOB SUMMARY: Provides professional clinical care for patients following established standards and practices. Prepares patients
assists patients and family members before, during and after a doctor's visit. Works under the direct supervision of the physician.
their scope of duties to the provider, Clinical Coordinator or Division Administrator.

JOB RESPONSIBILITIES:

- Prepare patients for examination and assists physician during treatment/procedures, examinations and testing of patients.
- Prepare, restock and sterilize examination rooms, procedure rooms, lab area and all other patient care areas per established p‍
- Record patients' medical history, health maintenance, and chief complaint.
- Measure, record and document vital signs.
- Where applicable, perform phlebotomy, injections and other specimen collection per established policies and procedures as di
- Educate patients by providing information and instructions as directed by the provider; answering questions.
- Maintains safe, secure, and healthy work environment by following, and enforcing standards and procedures; complying with l‍
- Sterilize medical instruments per established standards and procedures.
- Relay messages from patients and front office staff to providers.
- Represent office in a professional manner. Treat all customers, internal and external, in a courteous and cooperative manner.
- Participate in team activities and professional development activities.
- Attend required meetings.
- Perform other duties as assigned.

MINIMUM QUALIFICATIONS:

For the Medical Assistant, most everything with bullet points and beyond are keywords. Under the Job Responsibilities, the main thing to show on your resume is that you have experience doing those tasks and to show examples of how well you did those tasks.

The following samples also have bullet points and other markings. Review them and you'll probably realize that you see these all of the time. Remember, the key is to show these on your resume and follow up with examples.

 **CAREER**BUILDER

Staff Accountant

firstPRO • Cartersville, GA

Feedback

Posted 2 days ago

Job Snapshot

Full-Time
Experience - At least 3 year(s)
Degree - 4 Year Degree
$60,000.00 - $65,000.00 /Year
Food
Accounting

Job Description

Staff Accountant

firstPRO 360 is a professional recruitment firm that has been providing talented professionals with exceptional opportunities since 1986. We invest in building relationships with people and businesses to benefit the communities that we live and work in.

Our mission is to provide a seamless recruiting solution for both our clients and candidates. We take the time to gain an understanding of our clients' and candidates' needs and customize our recruitment process because each individual and company is unique.

Our client is currently recruiting for a Staff Accountant with experience with SAP. Candidate **MUST HAVE** a bachelors degree, in accounting or finance, and experience with a SAP, and ideally experience with multiple business units.

Outline and responsibilities will include:

- Prepare monthly GL reconciliations
- Handle all aspects of daily and monthly accounting functions
- Coordinate month-end close
- Complete intercompany eliminations
- Account reconciliations
- Review cash balances
- Monthly journal entries
- Annual financial audits

The right candidate will be required to work on a direct hire bases. The salary will depend on experience and can range from $50000 – 65000 on perm. Qualified candidates, please apply online. The location is Cartersville, GA

Job Requirements

General Accounting Duties

Recent experience with SAP

Advanced Excel

Help us improve CareerBuilder by providing feedback about this job: Report this Job.

in JOBS

Sign in   **Join now**

This job is no longer accepting applications.

Jobs   Companies   Salaries

📁 Job title, keywords, or company name   ✕   ⊙ Location   ✕   Find jobs

Enterprise SaaS Account Executive (Corporate Real Estate)- East ⇗

Accruent

Atlanta, GA, US

🗓 Posted 33 days ago

People also viewed

Job description

Accruent is looking for top performing sales executives who have experience selling enterprise software applications to a company's key decision makers for their real estate and facilities management solutions. The Enterprise Account Executive will be responsible for all activities related to revenue generation of the our product and services as related to their accounts in the Corporate Real Estate industry.

This is a hunting role that requires mastery of the entire sales cycle including relationships at every level and the ability to forecast accurately based on data. The Account Executive will generate new sales in the medium and large enterprise market focusing on real estate lifecycle.

Essential Duties & Responsibilities

- Continue to position Accruent as a leader in our business.
- Own the full life cycle of the sales process
- Generate business from existing and new customers while reaching annual sales revenue goals.
- Sell to multiple levels of decision-makers within larger, complex accounts.
- Maintain opportunity progress in SalesForce

Industry

Computer Software, Facilities Services, and Telecommunications

Employment type

Full-time

Experience

Associate

Job function

Sales,Business Development

in JOBS

Sign in   Join now

- Provide input to sales plans and campaigns.

- On a limited basis, act as a mentor to junior level Account Executives.

- Stay current on market conditions, needs and competitor strategies, goals and approaches.

- Develop and maintain a working knowledge of Accruent solutions.

Development
Real Estate Manager
Exaserv
Accruent jobs   Greater Atlanta Area · 9d

Atlanta, GA jobs

 Product Manager, Business Process Automation
The Coca-Cola Com...
Atlanta, GA, US · 9d

Knowledge, Skills & Abilities

- 3-5 years of experience

- Proven experience building pipeline in a hunting role and managing a complex sale.

- Bachelor's degree in Business, Communications, Engineering, or a similar discipline.

- Strong analytical skills, including market strategy, customer requirements and success factors, and a value based selling process.

- Ability to create effective, convincing sales presentations.

- Excellent written and verbal communication skills.

- Team leader with strong interpersonal skills.

- Detailed sales process knowledge.

- Travel as required (50-75%).

 Business Development Manager
VDart Inc
Greater Atlanta A... · 10d

 Enterprise Sales Director, Southeast
Roostify
Atlanta, GA, US · 9d

 Industrial Real Estate Manager
The Home Depot
2455 Paces Ferry ... · 10d

Turner Director, Workplace Strategic Planning
Turner (Turner Broa...
Atlanta, Georgia · 9d

 HCM Sales Executive
Thread HCM
555 North Point C... · 7d

About Accruent

Accruent is a global software company that helps organizations achieve superior performance by transforming how they manage their physical resources. Its innovative, industry-leading cloud-based software and services enable organizations to optimize all stages of real estate, facilities and asset management, from capital planning through to IoT-based monitoring and control. With a proven track record across two decades, Accruent has created the only integrated SaaS-based framework and reporting platform for full lifecycle physical resource management. More than 7,000 global customers depend on Accruent solutions to drive out hidden costs, extend asset lifecycles, protect their brands,

Asset Manager (Commercial Real Estate)
PeopleSuite
Greater Atlanta Area · 9d

 S Vice President - Development
Skanska
Houston, TX, US · 14d

.ıCInC Success Partner / Account Manager

Project Manager (PMO) in Atlanta, GA
at HUNTER Technical Resources

Job Description

Project Manager
Atlanta, GA

One of the nation's leading banks, our client offers you the opportunity to expand your skill set and achieve your career goals.

DESCRIPTION:
Responsible for supporting the project management needs of a business unit, division, or company-wide. Has an understanding of the business unit(s) and the operating systems that support them. Serves as the project expert defining and executing projects regarding various business initiatives. Prepares business cases including financials and success factors for proposed operating and/or product changes. May conduct pilot tests of proposed operating and/or product changes. Completes post-audit of business case after implementation is complete. Manages the most complex projects independently that cross multiple divisions, states and/or are corporate-wide initiatives. Acts as a change catalyst. Responsible for setting project priorities, establishing goals and strategies. Responsible for project results. May negotiate with outside vendors and interact with and be able to influence, senior management. May manage or provide guidance to other team members.

REQUIREMENTS
- 7 years of successful Project/Change Management experience
- PMP Certification
- MBA
- Deep knowledge of segments of Wholesale Banking
- Experience in internal or external consulting organizations
- Recognized as an expert corporate consultant in multiple disciplines
- Demonstrated ability to lead and coach others
- Strong knowledge of MS Office
- Bachelor's degree in a relevant field, or an equivalent combination of education

5/3/2018, 6:35 PM

Where

Atlanta, GA

city, state, country

Home   View All Jobs (1,749)

What

job title, keywords

Scrum Master in Atlanta, Georgia

| Apply Now |

Clearance Level Must Be Able to Obtain:

No Active Clearance Required

Suitability:

Agency Specific

Job Family:

Information Technology

Job Description:

We are seeking a certified Scrum Master to join our team in support of the CDC ISS DME - Public Health Surveillance Systems. We have a team of about 15 people working together to build and enhance several applications with strong backend data verification capabilities running on SQL server and other newer technologies. In this role, you will be the scrum master supporting the development of public health surveillance systems.

Position is for full time employment with CSRA and will be based at our Atlanta, GA office on Corporate Square. You can work a flexible schedule Monday - Friday around core business hours with the opportunity to telework 1 day a week once established and with manager approval.

RESPONSIBILITIES AND DUTIES:

- Serve as the Scrum Master – track backlog of tasks, ensure on task with sprints, organize sprint planning meetings for multiple initiatives and multiple applications each running 3 weeks sprint and releases approximately once every 2 months.

- Review and remove roadblocks to ensure timelines and deliverables are on target

- Draft system process flows

- Assist in performing QA of systems.

- Utilize knowledge of computer system capabilities, business processes, and workflow.

- Ensure tasks are being completed in a timely manner (aligned with sprints)

- Use JIRA and TFS to track status updates and create status reports

| Apply Now |

Share

Current Search Criteria

Scrum Master

Atlanta

Georgia

Clear All

Why Your Resume Isn't Working

Property Manager

| 3.6 | Related Company – Los Angeles, CA

Apply !

Job   Company   Reviews

Company Rating

3.6

Glassdoor Estimated Salar·

$57,000/ year $41k

Overview

Affordable housing laid the foundation of Related Companies and we continue to place a high priority on developing, acquiring an for this sector. In fact, over 60% of our 50,000+ residential apartment homes under our management are part of one or more affoi programs, and an additional 20% of these homes provide workforce housing.

In the area of acquisitions and refinancing, we pursue properties that meet one of the following criteria: Section 8 properties with contracts; Section 236 properties in need of rehabilitation; Section 42 LIHTC properties with expiring low-income restrictions; Se properties with loans that can be prepaid; or other assisted properties, including HODAG, HOME, federal or state-financed public

Many of the buildings we encounter are in need of substantial upgrading and preservation in order to continue to properly fulfill t tenants. Given our 42 years of experience in debt and equity financing – as well as our extensive management of government-assi are well positioned to buy out existing owners who lack the resources and experience to recapitalize and, therefore, wish to exit tl arena. In addition, with our extensive development experience, we bring the knowhow to expertly rehabilitate the units, thus assu viability of these projects for years to come.

Responsibilities

Your role with the company:

This Property Manager is responsible for the overall day-to-day operations of a affordable housing community. The Property Mar overall day-to-day operations of one or several properties including the supervision of office and maintenance functions in compli policies and procedures and all applicable Equal Employment Opportunity, Fair Housing and Human Rights statutes, as well as en: compliance with all and any applicable program regulations.

Daily Responsibilities:

- Supervise accounts payable/receivable.
- Understanding of Operating Statements and Financial Budgets is a must.
- Supervise all marketing, leasing and administrative functions for LIHTC and Project Based Section 8 property.
- Hire, train and evaluates all office/maintenance staff.

Property Manager

AMERICAN EXPRESS

[3.6]   **Related Company** – Los Angeles, CA

Apply I

Job   Company   Reviews

Benefits and features:

- Incentive bonus program
- Training and development programs
- Benefits including: Medical, Dental, Life & Disability, Paid Time Off, 401(K), Flexible Spending Accounts
- Employee Recognition & Wellness Programs.

Qualifications

Background profile:

- Two+ years supervisory skills.
- Strong leadership, organizational, administrative skills.
- Team oriented.
- Must be able to prioritize, handle multiple tasks and meet deadlines.
- Working knowledge of Microsoft Office.
- Strong financial skills.
- Good problem solving skills.
- Knowledge of Rent stabilization regulations, Section 8 vouchers, LIHTC, Project Based Section 8, Recertification and income ca

#cb

Related is an Equal Opportunity Employer

Get alerts to jobs like this, to your inbox. | Create Job Alert |

Suggested searches

Assistant Property Manager   Leasing Consultant

Community Manager   >   Regional Property Manager

Store Manager   Manager

Similar Jobs You May Like

Director of Online Faculty Development

Send   ☆ Save   APPLY

UNIVERSITY of West Georgia

Employer	University of West Georgia
Location	Carrollton, Georgia
Posted	Apr 17, 2018
Administrative Jobs	Academic Affairs, Other Academic Affairs Jobs
Institution Type	Four-Year Institution

Classification Title

Position: Director of Online Faculty Development

Division: Academic Affairs

Department: Distance Learning - eTuition

Nature of Work

The Director of Online Faculty Development will serve as the campus leader for advancing online teaching and learning at UWG and use a variety of online pedagogical and andragogical approaches and technologies to support academic excellence and online learning. The Director of the UWG Online Faculty Development Center must be able to work under tight deadlines with minimal supervision in a fast-paced, dynamic environment that demands high quality, creativity, and consistency. The Director must be able to lead campus-wide discussions about managing online enrollment and enhancing online student-centered approaches and service. This position is responsible for helping create and to operationalize the strategic mission and vision for the FDC and for continued online development at UWG. The director must be skilled at collecting data and continually assessing outcomes, in order to meet institutional goals, market demands, and the goals of Complete College Georgia. The Director is also responsible for the management and supervision of an instructional design team, student workers, and other staff as well as support services and training programs. The Director is responsible for closely coordinating with the Center for Teaching and Learning for shared training for faculty and greater outreach to departments and colleges as well as the Center for Adults Learners & Veterans and other external stakeholders. Demonstrated knowledge and understanding of both

Similar jobs

WUTV Temporary Production Coordinator

University of West Georgia

Administrative Assistant - Division of Health Sciences

Georgia Highlands College

Administrative Assistant - Dental Hygiene

Georgia Highlands College

current practices and emerging trends in the field of instructional technology, design, and distance learning is required. Must be QM trained with a background in managing quality assurance initiatives for online programs at the university level. Must be able to conduct training in online/blended learning, extensive research into best practices, self-study, and innovative approaches to educational delivery. Must be able to to pitch, conceptualize, develop business models, and help in the planning for new non-credit and for-credit online programs. Director will design and implement an idea generation, validation and experimentation process to foster and deploy novel online initiatives at UWG. Director will also measure traction of new ideas, communicate UWG's progress in solving online challenges, create templates to be used for new programs, create success measurement devices, and represent UWG at events and councils and to external and internal constituents.

Required Qualifications

All of this!

Master's degree; Proven project management skills; supervisory experience; experience working in a higher education environment, training, or online teaching is also required. Experience as an online student will also be considered. Quality Matters certification (or comparable), data collection, and assessment experience is required. Broad-based knowledge and skill in operating a variety of software applications used in multimedia, courseware development, Learning Management Systems, and SCTBanner or similar systems is required.

Preferred Qualifications

Doctoral degree in education, instructional design, instructional technology, media, business, management, or related subject; experience working specifically with the Desire2Learn learning management system.

Salary

$58,548 minimum - $83,856 midpoint

5/3/2018, 6:30 PM

≡

Published on www.newyorkfed.org | 07 Apr 2018

Federal Reserve Law Enforcement Officer Academy - September 2018 (Posting Expires on April 20, 2018)

🏛 Federal Reserve Bank of New York   📍 New York City, NY

The United States Federal Reserve Police serve as the law enforcement arm of the Federal Reserve System and they are responsible for providing police protection for the Federal Reserve System which is the Central Bank of the United States. Our sworn law enforcement Officers provide 24/7 protection of Bank property, personnel and valuables at our landmark headquarters in lower Manhattan. Our FLETA Accredited (Federal Law Enforcement Training Association) Basic Law Enforcement Course (BLEC) consists of an intense, highly regimented seven week rigorous physical and academic training program that includes formal legal and law enforcement classroom, firearms and scenario based training and testing

Participants must be able to graduate the Academy having met all requirements to become a Federal Law Enforcement Officer of the Federal Reserve System.   Salary: $48,000 Important notifications We recommend printing out this position description for your reference because it will not be available online after the posting deadline date

Do not apply from a mobile device because your resume will not attach

The recruitment database requires submission from a laptop or desktop computer to ensure that your application and resume are received

Please complete all fields when applying including the request to "cut and paste" your resume AND attach a copy

We require both steps to be completed

This Academy is training Officers for our New York City lower Manhattan location only at this time. Responsibilities of a Federal Reserve Law Enforcement Officer Physical protection of Bank property, facilities, employees, non-employees, and visitors by conducting interior and exterior patrols and manning highly visible surveillance posts in all weather conditions; Carry firearms and make arrests for offenses against the United States and accessing law enforcement information pursuant to section 11(q) of the Federal Reserve Act (12 U.S.C

248(q); Perform mobile patrols in marked and unmarked Federal Reserve Police emergency vehicles; Conduct diligent visual review and observation of all persons, vehicles and activity in the vicinity of posts or persons entering the facilities

5/3/2018, 6:42 PM

metroatlantajobs.com
Live here. Work here.™

Find a Job   Resources ▾   Employers ▾   Login/Register ▾

Home / Find a Job / Police Officer

Police Officer

Marietta, GA

Share in 🐦 f G+

Apply Now   ✉ Email Job

Job Description

Job Description

This is the first rank of the Marietta Police force that includes both non-certified and certified officers. Certified officers are expected to demonstrate competency in law enforcement procedures. Works under the general supervision of an assigned sergeant. Performs a wide range of law enforcement functions including making arrests, issuing traffic tickets, crowd control and investigative work to promote public safety and security, crime prevention and general enforcement of the law.

- Patrols assigned area to control traffic, prevent crime or disturbance of peace, and arrest violators as required. Officers will be issued various equipment to include a patrol car with radio, portable radio, various weapons, shoes and uniforms. Additional equipment will be issued for special assignments for bicycle patrol, narcotics units, forensic technician, detectives, K-9, STEP, etc.
- Identifies criminal offenders and criminal activity, and where appropriate apprehends offenders. Holds suspects and calls for back-up as needed. Participates in subsequent court proceedings as required.
- Responds to emergency dispatch including calls from citizens requesting emergency assistance in order to prevent injury, death, and/or damage to property. Calls out medical personnel as needed and provides emergency first aid, when necessary, until emergency personnel arrive.
- Provides assistance and backs up other officers as needed on dangerous calls. Holds suspects until prisoner transport unit arrives or makes transport themselves. Secures crime scene evidence and requests Field Evidence Technicians as needed.

Job Summary

Company
City of Marietta

🐦 f

Start Date
As soon as possible

Employment Term and Type
Regular, Full Time

Required Education
High School or Equivalent

Required Experience
2+ years

- Enforces state and local laws by arresting violators who commit misdemeanors and felonies. Keeps current with changes in laws impacting law enforcement procedures including attending seminars and formal training as required.
- Appears in city, state, and federal courts as a witness or to defend charges as appropriate. Provides incident reports and related evidence to prosecutors and attorneys as needed.
- Engages in traffic control activities which include responding to traffic accidents; issuing traffic and parking citations; conducting sobriety tests, directing and re-routing traffic around accidents, street hazards and congestion; assisting persons stranded on public roadways; dispatches emergency personnel and tow trucks to clear traffic congestion.
- Completes daily shift activity and incident reports as required. Completes all report records for performance and court proceedings.
- May be assigned apprehension and detection activities which include interviewing victims, witnesses, and other involved parties; collecting evidence; assembling composites, photos, and line-ups for suspect identification; communicating with other agencies to obtain additional evidence; and documenting actions with daily reports.
- May be assigned surveillance, undercover, for observation of unlawful activities.

Knowledge, Skills and Abilities
Preferred Requirements -
- High school diploma or GED.
- Must be at least 19 3/4 years of age at time of written exam) and a U.S. citizen (proof of U.S. citizenship at time of hire required).
- Must be fluent in the English language, (including reading, writing, and speaking).
- Must be able to pass a written entry examination, background investigation, and oral examination, polygraph examination, and drug screen.
- Must obtain a Georgia Peace Officer Standard Training certification (POST) by the end of working test period and maintain certification annually by attending at least 20 hours of POST approved training.
- Must be able to successfully pass a standard physical fitness exam, medical exam and drug screen, a polygraph exam, and psychological test.
- Must achieve and maintain certification in the use of firearms.
- Must be free of any felony convictions, domestic violence convictions, or sufficient misdemeanor convictions to evidence a pattern. Must be of good habits and moral character.

Additional Information
Entry Rate 1: $36,483 annually
New hires and current employees with HS diploma or
GED, and who are not GA P.O.S.T. certified.

Entry Rate 2: $38,313 annually

Medical Device Sales Rep - Leading Device Technology

Brett Fisher Group – Atlanta, GA

Apply I

Job   Company

Our award-winning, rapidly-growing medical device client produces a life-saving airway and respiratory drug delivery device sold patients in 75 countries worldwide. Their groundbreaking technology is a category leader. We are seeking an accomplished critica (regional sales leader) to oversee the Arizona and New Mexico territory. This role trains and manages relationships with distribut great transition into sales management. This is a great opportunity to join a well-established, rapidly growing, dynamic company v leadership.

What You'll Tackle:

- Responsible for achieving sales revenue budget for products within a territory.
- Drive and support the distributors in the U.S.
- Provide clinical training and support for customers and distributors.
- Launch new products in combination with marketing in the territory.
- Establish strong physician and clinician relationships.
- Possess value based and strategic selling skills.
- Be innovative in creating new sales opportunities for client products.
- Conduct peer to peer and promotional events in your territory.
- Any other ad hoc duties at the request of your manager.

What's Needed to Win:

- Bachelor's degree.
- 3+ years of experience in medical device sales; preferably in acute care settings; hospital, IDN, ICU, surgery center, emergency care call points.
- An accomplished sales leader and revenue builder.
- Previous engagement and sales experience with distributor partners, a strong plus.
- A dynamic, confident, driven and articulate individual who can interact effectively with all levels of the organization, forging hi communicating in a compelling and direct fashion.
- Ability to travel overnight at least 60% of the time outside of the Houston market.

Interviewing immediately.

Salary commensurate with experience.

Chapter 6

Using an Antiquated or Wrong Format

"This Looks Like Something From the '80s. Wait... It Is!"

I can't tell you how many times in a year I see people using that same antiquated left aligned template. I mean the one with all of the dates to the left, months and years of employment as well. If you are doing this, do yourself a favor and please stop! Get creative and make your resume stand out.

You can do so by doing the following:

- Center your headings

- List your dates to the right of the page. This is actually the modern way.

- List the years of employment only. Unless you're listing a position that's less than one year, then it's usually essential to list the months as well.

Using the wrong format can also make your resume appear overdone, flowery or full of fluff. Let's say you have a friend in graphic design who had their resume professionally written. So you ask your friend for tips. He welcomes you to take a look at his resume. They may have a logo or some nice touch that's suitable for their industry. In addition they have elaborate language throughout the document that makes them sound amazing! You on the other hand, are in a totally different industry where the tone would be completely different. You're not really certain if some of the words from his resume apply to you, but they sound good, so you decide to go with it.

What's Wrong With This Statement?

Star Grocery, Weston, NY   2016 – 2018
Stock Clerk
    1.Executed products into the store and later onto the shelves.

Notice how the word "executed" is used in the bulleted example above. Saying you executed or launched something when nothing in your particular role involved this is not impressive.

A better way of wording the sentence in the box above is shown below.

Star Grocery, Weston, NY   2016 – 2018
Store Clerk
    1. Stocked shelves with dry goods delivered from daily
       shipments.

Make sure the verbiage on your resume matches your particular job. Do not use fancy jargon that would be more suitable for a senior level executive of a Fortune 500 Company, or any other level that doesn't pertain to you. Industry leaders can spot a fake resume right away. Throughout my years of writing I have seen plenty of job candidates use incorrect or exaggerated language that simply does not apply to them. Many times a person will have a title of, let's say, Director, but it is just that, a "title" because they really don't have the responsibilities that a Director has. However, someone else may suggest they use elaborate language simply because it sounds good. As hiring managers, we know when you're trying to fake your way through. It's best to just go to the library, view a resume sample book, buy one or simply do an

Internet search and look at some resume samples to get an idea of what a resume for your targeted industry would look like.

Another example of using the wrong format is when you try to squeeze in every bit of detail about a position, making the resume cluttered or too compact. It is not necessary to tell your entire history or every single responsibility of your job since some things are a given.

What about where certain sections and headings should go? One we notice quite often is the Education heading. Students are taught in college to always list this first on the resume. Many continue to do so well beyond their college or entry-level years. The first items on a resume should show focus, usually done with a brief summary and/or related keywords section. If you are a new college graduate with very little experience in your field, and seeking an entry-level position, list the summary and keywords, then add the education section. The same usually goes for professionals who are actually in education as well. For other industries, and if you are well beyond your collegiate years, then the education information goes towards the end of the resume. The reason being is you need to get to the point of your experience and what you have to offer right away.

Many of our clients ask, "Which is better, a chronological or a functional format?"

The answer is it depends on your employment history and your goals. If you are a contract worker assigned to several projects in one year with different companies, using the chronological format may make you appear to be a job hopper. Plus, this could take up valuable real estate if you're listing your role and details for each position. A functional format would be better. By the way, in the Professional Resume Writing industry we create *showcase* formats, but for the sake of keeping the terms to the norm we'll say *functional*.

The difference is a showcase format showcases your skills and experience first and then the dates of employment. A functional format is similar, only it's mostly skills-based with a summary of your work history last. Some people even leave dates of employment off.

Another reason you may want to use the functional format is if you are trying to transition back to a former career. For example, if you are a schoolteacher and you were in IT sales several years ago. Maybe you need to show that although it was many years ago, you do have the skills necessary to go back into IT. Maybe you were a rock star in your previous IT life and you want to get this point across right away. You can simply put a heading that says "IT Experience" first, list your relevant roles and then the Teaching Experience next.

Here's a Partial Example:

JOHN A. SMITH

15115 John J. Delaney Drive, Charlotte, NC 28277

Cell: 704-566-9823 * johnsmith32@gmail.com

SUMMARY OF QUALIFICATIONS

Technically savvy professional with strong analytical skills seeking to transition back into the IT sales industry. Currently utilizing advanced technology in higher education, staying abreast of the latest trends in software applications.

Well versed in integrated software, applications for mobile devices and those for Windows and Mac operating systems.

PROFESSIONAL EXPERIENCE

IT Sales

➤ Ranked among the top five sales representatives at Digicom for a new proprietary smart phone app. Contributed to $1.5 million in company revenue for 2015.

➤ Trained a team of new field representatives assigned to the Samsung account.

➤ Gained extensive experience in SAP resulting in being selected for a major accounting firm account.

Teaching

➤ Led the implementation of new Smart Board technology into the classrooms at Rogers High School.

➤ Effectively trained a staff of 24 teachers on all aspects and features for creating lesson plans.

➤ Played an integral role in school being awarded $20,000 worth of new computers for the media center.

And after this you would list your education, any current technical skills, and your employment history with the company names, your titles and dates of employment. Notice this is similar to the chapter on targeted resumes where we highlighted that candidate's relevant experience to the job posting first. In this case, it's the same thing. Only it's for a transition. You can find complete examples on pages 88 and 115.

So now you've been presented with two reasons why you would use the functional format and how to implement it. If you have nothing that may look unfavorable to a hiring manager, then by all means choose the chronological format first. It's been said that most recruiters prefer this one anyway because your work history is easier to follow, and it shows you're not trying to hide anything.

Chapter 7

Who Wrote It?

Were there multiple people? Did your friends, mother, father, sister, brother and other relatives lay down the do's and don'ts or myths for doing your resume the right way? Did you even speak with a couple of different hiring managers? I mean, of course they should know, right? The problem again is that your friends and family only get part of it right. As for the managers, what may work for one hiring authority may not work for the other.

Decided to use a professional resume writer? Well, let's talk about that. I cannot stress enough how important it is to put your own voice to your resume. This is why if you have someone preparing it for you, he or she should always do a consultation, in-take, interview or whatever you want to call it, just as long as the person asks you some important questions to create the most effective resume possible. It's also important that *you* give them what they need.

Don't expect them to create something out of thin air. In other words, the writer can only create your resume based on what you give them. This person should also be very knowledgeable about your field. When I first started writing and critiquing resumes, I mainly did so for my coworkers who were in Customer Service and IT. Outside of them, I could help those in restaurant or banking which were my previous jobs. These were the fields I knew about, and I had been exposed to management as well. I suppose if someone from the Marketing or Implementation department came and asked me to assist them with their resume, I would have created a pretty decent document, but since that wasn't my area of expertise, I would not have known what questions to ask in order to sell them, or how to market them in the best light possible. Which goes back to what a resume is—a marketing tool.

Fast-forward to today and I've probably created a resume for virtually every traditional and non-traditional industry out there. Thanks to doing client assessments and consultations, I've learned what is vital for various industries. When necessary, I assign the project to someone who is more knowledgeable about an industry than I, or if I know enough for a "decent" resume, I'll do extensive research to make sure I create a fabulous resume! If I happen to stumble upon something that really doesn't apply to the client, of course they will let me know. I'll even go to hiring managers in their field, or maybe even contact the one in charge of the job posting or the recruiter. This is so I can gain clarification or to gauge what it is they are truly looking for in a candidate, so that I can put mine at the top of their list. Back in the day my friends weren't paying one red cent for me to write their resume. So of course, I wouldn't go through all of that for them, but for paying clients, I'll go to the ends of the Earth. Well, maybe not the ends, but I take a lot of time. I'll bet you never thought writers do all of that, huh? The ones who care do.

There are at least 600 plus resume writing companies out there. However, only handfuls are actual companies. Most of the websites you visit are people who are experienced in writing resumes, but *how much* experience they have is another question. And I don't mean just in your field as I mentioned above, but writing resumes on a daily basis and for how long. There are the Certified Professional Resume Writers who are dedicated to the craft and write regularly for a living. Others have day jobs and write on the side for extra money. And then there are those who work for resume mills—certified and non-certified writers.

Don't Let a Resume Mill Write Your Resume!

Or, I should say *someone* from a resume mill. What's a resume mill, you ask? It's a company that cares more about quantity than quality. Companies like this usually have you fill out a questionnaire listing additional information not on your resume. If you don't already have an existing resume they may have you practically write the new one yourself! They'll just format it nicely. Beyond the introductory free resume evaluation where they scare you into a do or die situation, a brief description of the company and their process, there is usually no more direct client contact once you're on board. Got a question? Email it. Just thought of something and need to speak to someone? Tough luck! You better brush up on your written communication skills, because from now on, it's just emailing back and forth.

Email is fine, but what if the context is all wrong and the only way you can really convey what you mean is by actually speaking to your writer? Oh, and if they have a question that they could probably understand better by calling you? Forget about it. They'll mark your resume with a hundred highlights before they'll call you. It's almost as if it's the writer's death sentence if they even try. Most resume mills don't actually let you speak with your writer by phone. They are paid to do one thing, and that's crank those resumes out like a GM assembly line.

Another problem with writers from these kinds of companies is they are not able to use their creativity to the fullest extent when it comes to formatting. They have to go with a template that the company requires them to use. And the writer, who is usually a sub-contractor not making much money per resume, has to write as many as they can to make a decent living. Or, they may be under contract to produce so many documents per week. And they *must* meet the deadlines or else no more work will be given to them. This can be very draining. A deadline-driven environment is essential; however, one without attention to detail, or just a carbon copy of all of the other job candidates' resumes out there, is doing a disservice to you, the client and the job candidate.

How Do You Spot a Resume Mill?

You see an ad for a free resume critique—the evaluation I mentioned. You submit your existing resume by email. You receive an email response back with the critique ripping your resume to pieces! The person who "maybe" just evaluated your entire resume has the goal of getting you to use their services regardless of whether you need their help or not.

You see the truth of the matter is, if you wrote the first one and you've used it in the past, you could probably do it yourself again. You may just need some tweaking here and there. I have seen plenty of resumes like this, so our team would not take them if there wasn't much more we could do to improve it. Unless of course the client insisted because maybe they just don't have the time, need our expertise in concise wording, a more modern format, etc... There are hundreds of job candidates who can't or have no inclination to write their own resume, but for the ones whose resumes don't look too bad, a writer from a resume mill will most likely have you thinking your resume needs surgery, *stat!*

This critique is also usually a standard canned response that's sent to everyone. Oh, they may change one or two lines to make it seem more personable, but it's the same old response they give over and over to each and every inquirer. If you don't believe me, just have your friend (someone in a different field) send their resume to the same company a few days later.

You may not even have the same problems as most job candidates they've seen. Suppose you know all about adding quantifiable accomplishments, but your resume simply doesn't give enough of a description of your daily role. Although a resume shouldn't list an encyclopedia of duties, the reader still needs to know *something* about what you do. Or suppose you're trying to transition into a new field, as I mentioned in the previous chapter. In this case, you may just need to refocus it and leave out non-relevant info. Again, if you simply do not know how to do this, nor have the time, that's fine, but the writer from the resume mill won't even point this out so that you'll at least know what they're going to do differently if you choose them to rewrite it. They'll just give you the canned response. Now I'm not saying they're all totally bad because I do know some good writers who worked for some of these companies, but you usually don't get the same kind of personalized attention. Most of them are cheap. Some people are okay with this. You decide.

So What Kind of Writer Should You Use?

If you don't have a friend or acquaintance who knows how to write the right kind of resume for you, then a Certified Professional Resume Writer (CPRW) is your best investment. One who writes resumes for a living and networks with recruiters on a regular basis. A writer with this credential has been through rigorous testing (think similar to the Graduate Management Admission Test or GMAT) in both resume writing and some basic testing regarding the employment industry. This includes which questions are legal for a hiring manager to ask, among other things.

Although it's a resume, for the many writers who do actually do an in-depth consultation, a lot of HR-related questions come up during and after the consultations. For example, how much to tell an employer about previous time off due to an illness or how to explain a sabbatical. You, the job candidate need advice on how to answer these questions.

Most CPRWs are members of a professional resume writer organization. This way they stay abreast on the latest trends through networking with other writers, former and current recruiters, and career coaches. They participate in webinars, career industry conferences, retreats and anything else that can help them to hone their craft. They are serious writers!

Now a CPRW may also work for a resume mill, but at least you'll have *some* comfort in knowing the person will be able to write effectively. Just be careful when doing your search. Whether it's a resume mill, one-man shop, college career counselor doing resumes on the side, or simply a small staff of writers and editors; once you do your online search for reviews (you didn't forget this, right?), make sure to ask questions such as: What is your success rate? Who will be writing my resume? What's the background of the writer? If you're speaking to the writer, ask to see samples of *their* particular work and if possible, a sample of a resume for your industry. Also ask about their policy for revisions and their guarantee. A good firm will provide a certain number of free revisions. If you're not satisfied, they will usually work with you until you are.

Some candidates prefer that the person doing their consultation is the one actually writing the resume. For some large or busy firms this is nearly impossible, and it puts entirely too much stress on the writer, but there are plenty of one-man shops out there who will do it all. There are some that have a good balance too. Some members of the staff can do a small number of consultations together with writing. With others you may work strictly with the writer after your consultation. Either way, it's always good for a firm to have a team of writers, editors, proofreaders and recruiters. The main thing though is that you get personalized attention and the most effective resume to paint you in the best light possible.

As I mentioned in Chapter 2, resumes can run as low as $10 a page (run if you see this!) to $500 or $600, but they can actually go up to $1000 or more. I know you're thinking, *I'll run if I see this!* Well, it's more than just a resume and they are very labor-intensive. Of course, it's a labor of love for those of us who love the craft, but still. You may think you just need some tweaking here and there, or to add your most recent position, or… as many will say a "basic" or "generic" resume. A Certified Professional Resume Writer who cares about the client, and his or her reputation knows there's just no such thing as basic or generic. And that tweaking or adding your most recent position can take a considerable amount of time, depending on the original format of the resume, the strategy used to market you, the research (yes some of us do a lot of research) and the editing involved.

Here are some normal rates for Certified Professional Resume Writers.

Mind you, many writers charge more depending on how long they've been in business, their experience level and the overall service they're providing.

New Graduate or Entry Level Candidate: $100–$200
Professionals, Non-Management: $200–$300
General Management and Executives: $400–$600
Senior, Director and C-Level Executives: $500–$1000+

These are just for the resume. Add on a cover letter or any other services and you could be adding another $50-$100 more per item. Now before you go into cardiac arrest, remember this is an investment in yourself. I remember once around 2007 a management level client balked at my $385 rate. This was back when everyone else was charging $400. Some of those same writers charge more now. (These have pretty much been the standard rates for nearly two decades now.) Anyway he blurted out, "Oh what the hell, I pay more than this for a pair of shoes!" Now, I was shocked. He was in sales. Several months later I saw him in a major magazine winning some award for the new company he was with. He invested in his career and it eventually paid off.

Many writers will reason that for every day you're not in your dream job—or don't even have a job—you're losing money. A professional resume written by a Certified Professional will open doors and opportunities, landing you closer to the salary you desire. Using the rates I mentioned above, I've seen professional writers break down the return on investment something like this:

New Graduate or Entry Level Resume: $100–$200

Annual Salary of the New Job: $45,000–$55,000

Professionals, Non-Management: $200–$300

Annual Salary of the New Job: $55,000–$65,000

General Management and Executives: $400–$600

Annual Salary of the New Job: $75,000–$125,000

I separated these last two since the salaries vary greatly.

Senior or Director Level: $500–$600

Annual Salary of the New Job: $155,000–$200,000

C-Level Executives: $700-$1000+

Annual Salary of the New Job: $300,000–$500,000+

Final note:

Remember when I mentioned that resume mills use certified and non-certified writers? Well, anybody can *claim* to be a Certified Professional Resume Writer, so it's best to ask some pertinent questions before you pay your money to one. Such as

1. Where did they obtain their certification from? For example which accrediting body or organization.

2. How long have they been in business and what is their success rate? Their website should state these things.

3. Do they guarantee their work? No over-promising either. About the most a writer should guarantee is that you will get interviews.

4. How do they handle revisions?

Remember These Tips:

1. Ask to see samples of their work.

2. It's always best to have the option to meet either in person or by phone. Not just the "fill out a form, send your resume and I'll get back to you" process.

3. Don't let the person pressure you or make you feel guilty if you don't order right then and there. As I said this is an investment, so you need to make sure you're choosing wisely.

4. If you're nervous or apprehensive, I can't stress this enough: **research, research, and do more research!**

5. Make sure you are ready to move forward with a positive attitude. It makes the working relationship between you and your writer so much better.

Last thing to remember:

A Cheap Resume is *NOT* Cheap!

Chapter 8

The Duty-Driven Resume and the Accomplished-Based Resume

Does the experience section of your resume look like this?

- Created documents and reports for senior management to conduct forecast analysis.

- Managed all employees, all recruiting, hiring, firing, training, scheduling, performance reviews, coaching, employee relations, incentive program and professional development.

- Handled customer service problems, changes or corrections in billing, refunds and new orders.

- Managed inventory, supply ordering, new orders for marketing, accounting and management.

- Sold products to new customers, current customers and got leads for new customers.

Okay, by now you get my drift, or at least I hope you do. It sounds a little boring, right? Repetitive maybe? As professional resume writers we see this all the time. Employers do want to know what you did; however, some things are a given and it's not necessary to tell your entire work history for that one job. A brief description is all that's needed. I understand some roles have a ton of duties, such as an Accountant with different levels, or maybe you wear several hats. Still, you can sum them up in a line or two, a small paragraph form, or use sections.

Let's say you're in the military and responsibilities spread across multiple units such as Joint Forces Command (JFCOM), Mission Operations Center (MOC) or Ministry of Defense (MOD).

Maybe it looks like this:

Serve as the senior enlisted advisor supporting the U.S. Army Central, U.S. Central Command (USCENTCOM) and U.S. Intelligence and Security Command (INSCOM). Oversee training, administration, readiness and professional development of 91 soldiers and civilians. Manage a wide range of HR procedures. Direct critical training events to maintain continuous operations throughout the USCENTCOM division. Act as NCOIC night shift guard for all personnel and full accountability for $15 million in equipment.

By the way, this was a lot lengthier before. I actually cut it down some!

Your brief paragraph may not be as brief as most hiring managers prefer with all of this, but if you have a lot of responsibilities that impact the organization, you may need to list them. If this is your case, just make them bullet points and then create a separate set of bullets for your accomplishments (make sure you are clear in your distinction between the duties and accomplishments) or split the paragraph in two. See these examples:

- Serve as the senior enlisted advisor supporting the U.S. Army Central, U.S. Central Command (USCENTCOM) and U.S. Intelligence and Security Command (INSCOM).
- Oversee training, administration, readiness and professional development of 91 soldiers and civilians. Manage a wide range of HR procedures.
- Direct critical training events to maintain continuous operations throughout the USCENTCOM division. Act as NCOIC night shift guard for all personnel and full accountability for $15 million in equipment.

Or again (my favorite), just split the paragraph in two:

Serve as the senior enlisted advisor supporting the U.S. Army Central, U.S. Central Command (USCENTCOM) and U.S. Intelligence and Security Command (INSCOM). Oversee training, administration, readiness and professional development of 91 soldiers and civilians.

Manage a wide range of HR procedures. Direct critical training events to maintain continuous operations throughout the USCENTCOM division. Act as NCOIC night shift guard for all personnel and full accountability for $15 million in equipment.

This works for federal government jobs of various GS levels, as well as traditional jobs with multiple responsibilities. Think HR and project managers. We have found that splitting up the paragraph and then going right into the accomplishments works best for our clients, no matter how much must be added to show the actual level of responsibilities.

Whether you use bullets or the paragraph form, you can make a better impact by quantifying your duties. This makes them interesting. Explain why you handled certain tasks, or simply use better wording. Using a couple of the above bullet examples from the first set, you can rewrite them like this:

- Developed quarterly reports for 10 senior-level managers to conduct their annual forecast analysis.

- Managed 15 direct reports and all related HR tasks, including recruitment, scheduling, training and coaching.

- Oversaw $300K worth of inventory consisting of high-end brands. Ensured adequate supply and managed the ordering for cross-functional departments.

Notice how the duties in the first bullet are quantified. The duties in the second one are as well and the duties have been somewhat summarized. And the last bullet not only quantifies the inventory, but also tells the type of inventory and which types of departments the ordering was for instead of listing each one. This makes it a more concise read.

Once you streamline your duties, you'll want to add ACCOMPLISHMENTS. This is something we stress often.

What exactly are accomplishments and what kinds should you add?

This is another question we often get during client consultations. We recommend *quantifiable* accomplishments; however, any results you can show, contributions you've made, goals you've achieved and pretty much anything that makes you fabulous, list it.

So should these be awards?

Not necessarily, but by all means add them if they're recent or if you think they'll help. For example, the President's Award, which is popular with many sales professionals, always looks good whether it was this year or five years ago. Of course if it was a few years ago you would need to add more recent accomplishments as well. Examples of accomplishments, results, contributions and other ways you can show you're a value to the company would be:

- Earned The President's Circle Award consistently every year from 2008 to 2016.

- Successfully managed an increase of 20% more workload due to cutbacks in the marketing department.

- Generated $15 million in sales last year; the highest in company history for a single department.

- Ranked among the top associates in the district for surpassing all company goals and deadlines.

So there's a mix here of quantifiable and non-quantifiable accomplishments. Saying you're the best when you made your contribution and why you're a great asset will always suffice and make for good interview discussions.

Be Careful When Adding Accomplishments

Too many can be just as bad as not enough, and only listing accomplishments without anything else can also send your resume somersaulting to the slush pile. Why? For the following reasons:

1. **A hiring manager may not believe you.** If you start your experience section off with a load of bulleted accomplishments with no lead-in as to what you do (and again, it can be brief).

2. **They sound like everyone else's.** Especially those sales accomplishments, so again, they may sound unbelievable.

3. **They don't show "how" you achieved A, B, C...** Anyone can throw impressive numbers on their resume, but make them believable by showing *how* you achieved that number.

4. **Your resume doesn't tell a story.** The experience section really helps in telling the story for each of your positions. Help the employer get to know you a little. You can briefly describe how you moved through the ranks, or why you were hired and then how you succeeded. See the following example.

Dollar General Stores
District Manager, 2013 – Present

Recruited to a struggling territory to improve sales and profitability. Charged with overseeing 12 locations consisting of 220 employees throughout metro Atlanta. Established goals for each location, led training, and monitored operations along with GM performance.

* Restructured operations for three underperforming locations, resulting in a complete turnaround in sales within two months.

* Played an integral role in 5 of 12 GMs earning promotions and relocations to higher volume stores.

* Implemented a new employee incentive program that reduced turnover by 30% and increased performance by at least 20%.

Notice how the summary is shorter—just a brief lead-in. The accomplishments aren't all quantified either. The role of the District Manager in this case is more about overseeing operations, less about making individual sales; yet ensuring the stores achieve *their* sales and operational goals. Many candidates think if you don't have dollar amounts or awards to list then your accomplishments won't stand out.

Some companies simply hand down the rules and you just don't have a lot of control over things like implementation and sometimes it's the manager who keeps your individual sales stats, not you.

When all else fails and you simply have a brain freeze, think of yourself as just the worker bee, and you have no idea of what constitutes as accomplishments, then turn your duties around! Whether you're pushing paper or a broom day and night, there's a reason why your employer is keeping (or kept) you around. See the example below using two of the bullet points from the first set of duties:

- Created documents and reports for senior management to conduct forecast analysis.

Rewritten as:

- Successfully created documents and reports; delivered in a timely manner for senior executives to perform their forecast analysis.

- Managed all employees, all recruiting, hiring, firing, training, scheduling, performance reviews, coaching, employee relations, incentive program, and professional development.

Rewritten as:

- Showed exemplary leadership when managing employees, training and all related HR tasks.

- Implemented a highly effective employee incentive program that significantly reduced turnover.

Notice I added new wording and deleted some wording as well. *And yes, I split the one bullet in two for better impact.*

How Many Bullet Points Should You Add?

Another belief that I've noticed from some of our clients is they think you need to add a certain number of bullet points for accomplishments and that the number of bullets should be the same for each position. Well, this isn't always possible when you get to a company from way back when, or it was a temporary position where you really didn't do anything measurable, or…you simply can't remember much.

A good rule of thumb is to add at least three and no more than eight bullet points. Although, if you're adding a job from years ago and let's say you only have two bullets that's okay too. The hiring manager may not even make it that far back, or if it's non-relevant information from the ice ages, it won't matter much anyway, which brings me to the next chapter: Get to the good stuff!

Chapter 9

We Need You to Get to the Good Stuff Now!

"We don't have all day. Got golf to play!"

Do any of these situations apply to you? You're in a career transition, transitioning back to a former field; however, all of your related experience was several years ago.

You're in a new position, a promotion actually, but you've only been in the position for less than a year, so you really don't have any quantifiable accomplishments yet.

You're trying to go into Project Management, IT Management or any other management position. Although you've been serving in one of these roles for years, you've never actually held the title and you don't know how to get that across to someone.

You've just relocated from a big city to a smaller one for family reasons. What was a popular field (and the majority of your experience) in the big city is non-existent in this new one. Let's say it's the music industry, acting, high fashion or the like. You decide to use your transferable skills in something else.

For example, if you were in the music industry and you were over artist promotions, maybe you plan to look for a marketing position with an entertainment company, amusement park or any organization seeking your skills in branding and development. But… all of your experience was in the music industry, which is non-related.

Well have no fear! There's a way around any of these situations to show your worth.

If you're transitioning back to a former field and your experience is dated, you can do the following:

1. Mention one or two of your greatest accomplishments from way back when at the beginning of your resume in a summary.

2. List bullet points of your related experience with examples. If the companies were large Fortune 500 companies now is the time to name drop.

3. When you're doing #1 or #2 don't mention the dates, just the experience. Yes, if an employer asks you may have to go into detail, but the idea is to first get in front of him or her for an interview. You want to at least show that you have the experience right away. If it's towards the bottom of the second page or so many years ago, they may not even view it.

4. Follow up with a cover letter. This would be the best time to explain the transition, tell how you've stayed abreast of changes in the industry, studying and staying current with technology and anything else that wouldn't necessarily go on the resume. By the way, you can also:

Add relevant skills in a section by itself. You can title the section Core Competencies, Core Skills, Areas of Value, Knowledge and Abilities, or any suitable heading.

If you've only been in the position for a limited time with no quantifiable accomplishments or results. Try this:

1. List your goals and the projected date of completion or if you're on track for achieving these goals. For example, if your goal is to generate $2 million in sales by the end of the quarter and you're on track just say so! If you're working on a large development that is to be completed by the end of the year then again, say so. You can say something like:

On track for completion by Nov…or whatever the deadline is.

2. Tell how successful you've been in working towards the goals in other ways. If you lead a team talk about how effective you are by keeping everyone on one accord and ensuring they remain accountable. Do any training? Mention that.

3. Maybe you're in customer service or have to provide customer resolutions. Talk about how effectively you do this.

4. If you were hired to solve a problem or hand selected by the CEO lead into describing your role this way. It's very impressive.

When all else fails, just list your responsibilities similar to the example in the previous chapter where you quantify them, or tell how successful you are. Think about your unique attributes or skills that enable you to do a good job.

Trying to actually get the title for a role you've already been serving in for some time? This is very common for people trying to go into management or any specialist role. Many times the employer will have you do all of the work, but hold off on giving you the actual title, so they don't have to pay you for said title. On your resume, start off by describing your responsibilities with an emphasis on your leadership skills.

For example, if you're always leading special projects you could say:

- Manage special client projects from beginning to end.

Then follow it up with bullet points of the kinds of projects and results. Such as:

- Successfully led the Niamoka billing research project for two months resulting in $25,000 of uncollected revenue.

If you've solved problems as a technical expert, a specialist or any other role, mention it. And don't forget to follow it up in a cover letter with something to the effect of *although my actual title was not a _____* (enter position) *I was highly successful in….* (go into detail about the role).

And lastly, you've just relocated to another city where there are no jobs in your previous field. You can:

Show your transferable skills. Whatever the job posting says for the description of duties, skills and requirements, mention your transferable skills or accomplishments either in the beginning of the resume in the summary or right away with your most current position. Remember to watch for those "Must Haves" though. Using the example of the music industry to market your transferable skills in a completely different field, let's say the role is for brand development, and you previously did artist promotions for Sony. You could tell how successful you were in getting a particular artist the exposure they needed to increase record sales with campaigns you put together. Describe how quickly you delivered results.

The idea is to show that although it was a different field, you delivered measurable results for your previous employer; therefore, you can do the same for the next one, regardless of the industry. And again, include those details in a cover letter.

By the way, this is exactly what we did for some clients of ours when the music industry started restructuring and laying off people during the recession.
It worked!

Check out the following resume sample for one of our music clients. We created a showcase format for her to apply for marketing jobs; however, they were in other industries. Please note that everything including the client's name, artists' names and more have been changed to protect her and the actual clients she had. You'll notice we put her extensive years of experience, but this was only because the companies she targeted welcomed at least 10 or more years of experience.

CHINA RAYNER

356 South Hambra Cr. | Miami, FL 33156 | 315-225-4422 | chinay2@gmail.com

MARKETING EXECUTIVE
16 Years of Proven Success in
Promotions, Packaging, Branding and Developing Household Names

Award winning and creative Marketing and Promotions Specialist with a verifiable track record for generating compelling campaigns which ignite revenue; boosting sales to unprecedented numbers as evidenced by a successful career in the music industry. Able to identify profit growth areas and develop cohesive teams to capitalize on opportunities and reach organizational goals. Areas of expertise include:

* Targeted Marketing * Presentation & Closing Skills * Project Management
* Consumer Spending Trends * New Product Launching * Staff Management
* Promotional Tour & Event Planning * Team Training & Development * Sales Analysis

HIGHLIGHTS OF CAREER EXPERIENCE

Universal Music Group & RCA Records

- Served as Regional Promotions Manager and successfully directed marketing campaigns for youth-focused brands such as Miley Cyrus, SZA, Julia Michaels and Khalid; essentially supporting Universal's go-to-market strategy.
- Generated a significant amount of airplay and heavy rotation, by developing strong relationships with key directors and decision makers at 30 mainstream and crossover radio stations across the Southeastern US.
- Contributed to Khalid's sales of more than 1.5 million albums immediately after release date.
- Played a key role in generating SZA's worldwide exposure and Julia Michaels' crossover appeal propelling this artist to a household name.

Warner Bros. Records
- Spearheaded V-103's Soul Session promotional party for Dani Leigh's new album release which boosted download sales to 100,000-150,000; debuting in the top 10 during the first week.
- Performed heavy new artist development as a Marketing & Promotions Specialist with listening sessions, parties and special live performances in the major Atlanta market of Georgia, Alabama and Florida.

Continued on Next Page…

- Promoted Muse's single "Dig Down" by distributing customized CDs featuring Muse on backpacks to numerous radio station program directors. Also garnered media exposure through cocktail receptions, listening party invitations and trip giveaway incentives.
- Secured an unprecedented amount of airplay for Selena Gomez's "Same Old Love" resulting in record-breaking sales and a vacation to Italy.

SELECTED AWARDS

Achieved gold and platinum plaques for contributing to a million plus in sales for the following artists:

- Rihanna: 2012 – 2017
- Beyoncé (solo career): 2009 – 2010
- Taylor Swift (country): 2007 – 2008
- Ruben Studdard: 2004 – 2005

Additional Plaques and Awards

- The Sony Music/BMG Entertainment, Inc., Southeast Branch of Atlanta Contribution to the "Distributor of the Year" awards. Received awards for outstanding achievements in sales, promotions, marketing and merchandising from 1997 – 2002.
- Atlanta's Annual Million Dollar Music Conference awards.
- National Promotions Director, Sony Urban Music Department at Epic Records: 2001.
- Promotions Executive of the Year, Black Radio Exclusive Magazine: 2001.

EMPLOYMENT HISTORY

RCA Records   2008 – 2017
Independent Regional Promotions Manager

Universal Music Group   2002 – 2008
National Director, Urban Promotions   2004 – 2008
Marketing & Promotions Specialist   2003 – 2004

Warner Bros. Records   2002 – 2003
Marketing Assistant

EDUCATION

University of California, Los Angeles (UCLA)
Achieved 13 hours towards Masters degree in Marketing
University of Miami: FL
Bachelor of Business Administration

Another note about the cover letter is you can list what the job posting is requiring and then add bullet points to your related experience. If it says: *We're seeking someone who can lead a team in a high volume call center environment,* then give an example of when you led a team, how many team members, what you led them to do and the company name. By the way, at the end of this book there is a cover letter example. I put it in the back because it's in a cover letter section with a guide on how to write one.

Other Ways of Getting to the Point Quickly

It's not only about showing your skills, experience and accomplishments right away, but also about *how* you show them. Here are a few not-so-thrilling things we've seen on resumes that make the reviewer miss the important things because they just don't have enough time to wade through the bad:

The summary is too lengthy. Some hiring managers don't even care for a summary if it's for a non-management position. Since you may not know who will or won't like a summary, it's best not to make it too long. Others include,

Too many bullet points for a position (as mentioned earlier).

Lengthy bulleted items consisting of four lines or longer.

Too many paragraphs or a lengthy paragraph describing a position.

Every single duty listed before any accomplishments.

Duties and accomplishments mixed in together, so the accomplishments are hidden.

Education listed that's non-relevant or extra courses from several years ago.

Non-related accomplishments added because you are so proud of them.

You want to make sure it doesn't take until the second page before you show your most current position. If you're in education and you're trying to show all of your degrees, certifications and continuing education credits, or if you're in Information Technology trying to show all of your technical knowledge and certifications, by no means should you list all of this on the first page if it's going to draw the attention away from your experience and accomplishments, which need to be shown sooner rather than later.

SECTION II

Things to Overcome and/or How to handle them

Chapter 10

Red Flags!

"Ummm… Explain this. You know I'm side-eyeing you now, right?"

You want to make the recruiter or hiring manager's job of reviewing your resume as easy as possible. If you don't, it's on to the slush pile. If they have to try and figure out what, why, when and where, they'll just keep it moving, on to the next candidate.

What are red flags? They're the things on your resume that raise suspicion or make you seem like a less qualified candidate. You may think that you're one of the best applicants for the job. After all, you meet all of the qualifications, but even one red flag can knock you out of the running. Below are 11 examples of red flags on a resume:

1. Job-hopping

2. Gaps in employment

3. A P.O. Box instead of your home address

4. Not adding an address at all.

5. Adding your address, but no zip code in a city with the same street name for multiple areas (like Atlanta)

6. A non-professional email address, or the email address listing your side gig or hobby

7. Using an email address that you share with your spouse

8. A disconnected or an old telephone number where you can no longer be reached

9. Spelling errors or blatant grammatical mistakes

10. Claims or accomplishments that sound too good to be true

11. Positions listed with no dates at all, anywhere

Some of these sound ridiculously obvious, right? Well, you'd be surprised by what people tend to forget when they get busy, move around or have everyone in their ear telling them different ways to craft their resume. **Now let's go into detail...**

1. Job-hopping. There are a few industries where you're actually expected to hop from job to job. The entertainment industry, construction, freelancing and IT contracting jobs come to mind. They're usually projects (we used to call these gigs) that you work for a few days, weeks or months and then go on to the next one, but there may be some lag time in between.

For most traditional jobs today this is a no no! It does not look favorable at all. I used to give job candidates the benefit of the doubt whenever I saw this on a resume. I used to reason that for some people it just takes time to find the right fit, their spouse or parent was in the military, they got laid off, they were a contractor and the assignments were short. After all, we were in a recession once (or twice) right? Well, not anymore. I rarely hire freelancers. I used to say I wouldn't be like other hiring managers, who won't hire job hoppers; but now, well... let's just say if I see job hopping on your resume, I'll likely move on to the next one. And this is what most employers do these days—keep it moving. Especially if they're trying to keep their employee turnover low and want to keep paying a good salary.

Companies want loyal team players, not someone here today for a quick paycheck and gone tomorrow. I'm speaking for all hiring managers... we do not like spending all of that time and money training you only to find out you have an attendance problem, you're always ill, fickle about your career goals, so you hop here and there and so on.

So you may want to think about it before you say, 'I quit!' to the next employer for something trivial. Take the job seriously and show some stability. Now, I have known of companies who went through two or three mergers within a short time span and laid off all their employees. If you're ever caught in the crossfire, of course you can't help that. In the event that this happens to you there are a couple of things you can do: Don't list every single job you've had, or create a hybrid of a reverse chronological/functional format (what we call a showcase format). That way there's not so much attention drawn to your dates of employment. Or, you can do a combination of A and B.

2. Gaps in employment. Took some time off to go back to school? Then you better fill in that time off from work with the education. Think your volunteer work doesn't count since it wasn't paid? Add it anyway. Fixed your friends' computers on the side for little of nothing during the time you were looking for work? Add it! Got a side hustle? Add that too. I don't care how menial you think it is. Does this sound odd? Well, let's say your dates look like this:

TBN, Houston, TX 2014 – 2016

Frito-Lay, New York, NY 2005 – 2011

Or the last date of employment was 2013. You see the gap? Someone is going to question this. Even if you're working somewhere else where you're the star employee and the gap was years ago. I have heard plenty of times that a candidate was not called back because of this. So it's better to put something in that space rather than nothing at all.

3. Using a P.O. Box instead of your home address. If you remember, this is Myth #10 from the beginning of this book. Back in the day people would use a P.O. Box instead of their home address on a resume to keep scammers away and for various personal reasons. Although some people still do this, the latest trend now is to leave off your address entirely and just list your name, email address and telephone number. Or some people will put the city and state, but not the street number, street name or zip code. I've also seen resumes where people only listed the city, state and zip code. There are a number of reasons why, such as scammers, they're not living in the city where the job they're applying for is located just yet, but plan to move once they get the job, or they live many miles away from the area they're looking in and don't want the employer to discount them. This one seems to be the most common.

Well, I'm here to tell you it doesn't always work. In fact, I rarely see it work. I've seen some people get their foot in the door, which is of course what you're trying do, right? And you plan to explain your location during the interview. The problem is you may very well get your foot in the door, but if you live too far from the job, the employer will find out anyway. There's no law against a recruiter having you fill out an application listing your address, or asking what your address is so they can fill it in for you on the resume, or add to their employee or candidate database. And a P.O. Box just looks so unprofessional and unstable, or like you're hiding from someone. You're not hiding from someone, are you? Never mind, that is your business. I'm not judging. Ever wonder why you go through a series of interviews, even get a start date and then are told (sometimes the day before) that they went with someone else? Think about it.

Just know that a lot of hiring managers will assume when you leave your address or zip code off, but add the city and state, that yes, you probably live too far. And although this is also a red flag, would you rather raise a bigger flag by not adding your address at all, or only list the city and state? You can always add somewhere on the resume or even in a cover letter that you've had stellar attendance for all positions held (if this is the case) or that you have reliable transportation (in the cover letter), that you're always on time regardless and are not bound by geographical location. Note: *I'm talking about when you're applying directly to the employer.*

For conducting your job search online you'll either post it to a job search engine's resume board or a company's resume board. If you're worried about unscrupulous eyes viewing your resume when using any of the popular boards like Career Builder, Monster, Indeed, etc... then you can choose the anonymous feature that only shows your email address. This helps with the scams and spam emails. If you're using social media, you shouldn't list your address anyway. For example, with LinkedIn you just fill in the fields. There's no place or need to add your home or mailing address.

Lastly, if you are adamant about not using your mailing address, yet still want to look professional, get a UPS box. With this you'll have a regular street address with a PMB (Private Mailbox Number), but you can change the PMB part to just #1234 or Unit 1234. And besides, it's highly unlikely an employer is going to mail you anything before you're hired.

4. Not adding an address at all. Well, I guess this goes without saying with everything I've said so far about using a P.O. Box and partial addresses. If you don't add any address at all, the hiring manager is definitely likely to think you don't live in the city or near the city where the job is.

Note: Remember, it's when you're emailing, posting directly to a company's resume board, or giving your resume directly to a company or hiring manager that I recommend having your address listed. Also if you get the interview, make sure it's printed on your additional copies, which you should carry with you at all times anyway.

5. A non-professional email address, or the email address listing your side gig or hobby. I have seen some ridiculous looking emails through the years. Others weren't bad, but they just weren't professional or said too much. Like if you have a side business or hobby and your email address is something like: tonyscakes2013@yahoo.com, hangliderjoe@gmail.com, or joylovestowrite@comcast.net. If these have nothing to do with the jobs you're seeking, then don't use them on your resume. It's best just to use your first and last name, first initial and last name or some variation that's easy to remember and looks professional.

6. Using an email address that you share with your spouse. Now, for whatever reason I used to see this a lot between 2005 and 2010. Email addresses like mikeandkatie@msn.net, or themillers@yahoo.com. I see it less often these days, and when I do it still baffles me just as much as it did years ago. For the life of me I cannot figure out why in the world someone who's looking for a job would use a shared email address… with his or her spouse. I'm guessing when the person originally set it up, it was for household purposes. Maybe so both can keep track of bills that come in. Or, maybe it's also so spouses can look out for each other. If you're one of these people, *STOP*. It's just… unprofessional. The job search is supposed to be for you to conduct and you alone. You should be able to keep track of your own searches, answer your own emails and so on. An employer may wonder, *Will he get the email or will she*? Does the spouse not trust him? Also when you do this you're opening yourself up to personal information that you don't necessarily need to tell. What if some employers prefer single people or someone who can relocate or travel extensively if necessary? If they see you're married or have a partner they may think, *Hmmm, I wonder if he/she has children too.* Wouldn't you like to learn more about the job and decide if it's worth relocating or traveling once a week if necessary? Remember, you don't want to give employers a reason to weed you out. Something as simple as that shared email address may do just that. I'm just saying.

7. Using a disconnected or an old telephone number. This is rare, so I don't feel the need to elaborate much on this, but it's another thing I've encountered a few times when I've done my own phone screening. Usually with younger candidates, or those who haven't really looked at their resume in a while and rushed to post it out there. You know when an employer or an interviewer calls you with a few questions to narrow down who will be called for an actual interview? Depending on whether I have time or not (or what kind of mood I'm in), I may follow up with an email if the number I call is incorrect. Usually, the candidate will call me right away apologizing that they forgot to update the number. Most employers may not be as forgiving. They'll just, as I always say… keep it moving.

8. Spelling errors, blatant grammatical mistakes or weird formatting on your resume. I know we're only human (I've had to make several edits before), but remember this is your marketing tool and you need to put your best foot forward by presenting the most professional document possible. Using words in the wrong context, for example *their* when you meant *there* or misspelled words simply make you look lazy. And you may not be, it could be a simple mistake. However, to a hiring manager it shows that you're not taking your job search seriously, or that you don't pay attention to detail. This says a lot about how you may perform on the job. And don't just rely on Microsoft Word's spell check or Grammarly. Do use spell check; I'm saying this shouldn't be your only tool. Word doesn't recognize fragmented sentences, so there are plenty of instances where it will underline bulleted statements or words with another suggestion when you know it's correct, but then you doubt yourself. Like I said in the beginning, The Gregg Reference Manual is a great guide to keep on hand. Use it especially when you get into a bind.

A Few Words on Formatting

Be careful with the following:

Using templates. I hate those manufactured ones myself because they tend to shift. At BluePrint Resumes & Consulting, we create all documents from scratch, so we don't have to worry about this.

Extra spacing between words. For instance when you right align something to make the edge of the lines look neat.

Using tables and columns. If you're not familiar with these, don't use them. They can shift too or split words up on different lines, make things uneven and your sections can start to look messy.

Color, graphs and all that other fancy stuff. See Myth #9. These should be used sparingly. We did recently have a conference where a career industry expert said infographic resumes are the future, but even when and if they do become popular, they won't be for everyone. Today, we use color sparingly. We add charts for sales professionals when we think it's appropriate and other creative things, but we do so in a way that's very inviting. So again be careful. Better yet, this may be when you just want to hire a professional resume writer, or professional resume marketer, as they're moving towards calling us now. That's another book altogether.

9. Claims or accomplishments that sound too good to be true. Anything you put on your resume you'd better be able to prove or elaborate on it if you're asked about it during an interview. Don't just say something because it sounds good. Of course this should go without saying, but you'd be surprised by how many people say to me, "Yeah, that sounds good!" indicating to me what was stated wasn't actual fact, or "Yeah, say three years (versus one), my supervisor is cool and he'll back me up." But what if the person confirming your dates of employment during the reference check was from HR and simply going by your files?

10. Positions listed with only some dates, or no dates at all. A true functional resume has your experience, but no dates listed. Having only some dates for a chronological resume raises suspicion too. It definitely says you're hiding something. If you're trying to eliminate the job hopper appearance, re-read some of my previous tips. If your experience was a long time ago and you've been out of the workforce for a while, remember to fill in the gaps with *something* constructive. Some people have a series of jobs during a certain timeframe that was just so long ago it's embarrassing. For example, suppose from 1975 to 1990 you received a series of promotions and they absolutely speak to a certain skillset. You can just sum up these positions and list the latest year. You don't have to list them all. Here's an example:

Served in a series of customer service roles and promoted to management in 1990.
What if your profession does not even exist anymore? In this case it's best to just leave it off the resume.

End of Red Flags!

The following are other things that can keep your resume from working for you and tips on how to overcome possible shortcomings.

Chapter 11

Age Discrimination

We don't want our parents working here. Just someone we can mold. You know, someone who will bow down to us.

Yes, although the Age Discrimination Employment Act was enacted in 1967 (Wow! Even before I was born!) to promote employment of older workers based on their ability rather than age, well... age discrimination is REAL. Oh, it's against the law for an interviewer or hiring manager to actually come out and ask how old you are, so a common practice is to use the application and resume for clues. Before you run out and get cosmetic surgery done to make yourself look years younger, so you can get hired (yes, this was a trend), let's try working on what I call un-dating the resume, since there are several things that can date you (or make you appear older than the desired age).

Older applicants in their mid to late 40s, and 60s have to be especially careful in telling too much on a resume. The following are some of the quickest and sure-fire ways to date yourself on this important marketing tool. This is actually taken from a blog I wrote back in 2012, revised in 2016 and re-blogged about in 2018. You see? Even after all these years it still hasn't stopped, so it's necessary to keep rehashing this. Take a look at the 10 things that can date you and how to handle them.

1. Your Email Account Provider- Still have a Hotmail, AOL or EarthLink account? You can still keep it for personal emails if you like, but for job searching, *get rid of it*! Recruiters say this makes you look old. Better to get with the times and create an email address using Comcast, Gmail or another current service provider for job purposes.

2. Age in Your Email Address- Remember the red flag I mentioned in the previous chapter for a not so professional email address? Well, it's also a red flag if you have your age listed in your address. How about the year you were born? This still tells your age. And it's a huge red flag! You're telling the recruiter or hiring manager right away that you're 45, 55, 65, etc.... Oh, you think because you're younger that they'll be eager to see 1993 in your email address? Well, all employers aren't so eager. They may feel like you're too young and inexperienced. You never know who will frown at this and toss your resume right in the trash without even seeing that you qualify for the position in other ways; the ways that should matter most.

3. Your Middle Name- Listing your middle name on a resume is not only antiquated, but depending on the name itself, it can date you. For example a name like Oscar, Walter, Henry, Jean, etc... and if your first name *and* middle name sound old fashioned that's a double whammy! Of course you could be young and maybe your parents named you after a grandparent, great uncle/aunt, etc...That's nice, but just use an initial instead, or better yet just leave it off period. A first and last name will suffice and it's more memorable. Think of it this way, what do your coworkers remember you by? Rob A. Wallace over in IT or Rob Wallace over in IT? If you have one of those common names like John White, then you might want to add your middle initial. Now, if your first name sounds old fashioned well... just hope it's overlooked.

4. Adding a Suffix After Your Name- Skip the Jr., Senior, II, III, and so on. Unless you're applying for a job at the same company as your father, there's no need for this. It can raise suspicion as to how old you are. Even if you live in a rural area where this is still commonly done, it's better to just leave it off.

5. Adding Positions Beyond 20 Years- Especially if you go as far back as the '80s. The rule of thumb is to add the last 10-15 years on a resume. Well, most say 10, so we try our best to stick with 10 for our clients, but in many instances it's necessary to go back just a little further. What if you've been at your job for 20 or more years? This is very common. What if a job requires more than 10 or 15 years of experience for a trade? The best thing to do is to list the last 10-15 years with your titles (assuming, well hoping, you've had some promotions, led projects or something) and most notable accomplishments. When it comes down to it, you will have to state to the interviewer your actual dates of employment, but the idea is to get your foot in the door first.

6. Stating Many Years of Experience At The Top of the Resume- Yeah, you would think stating those 25 years or so would make you stand out, but no. Instead of making you more desirable, it raises red flags, like how quick (or slow) you are, can you multitask, take direction, will any health issues come up, and so on. Even saying *More than 18 years of experience in...* can be a concern. Unless, of course, the job posting is asking for at least 18 or more years. There are many postings that only specify 5 to 10 years of experience.

Some job candidates think that if they have and show more than what a posting says, this will make them more marketable, but in today's times that's not usually the case. Now, I have seen some industries, such as the insurance industry, where depending on the position more years are favorable. In IT there are many companies who will appreciate years beyond 15. Just to be safe, though, only add this if the hiring manager already knows you, or knows the person who referred you who may have already put in a good word for you. Or, as in the example with our music industry client, the postings or companies you're applying to actually state they prefer or welcome more than 10 or 15 years of experience.

7. Adding old company names- Do you remember American Bell, Southern Bell, Bell South, Pacific Bell, and a host of other *Bells?* Yes, those older names from the '90s and further back. So many companies have merged and changed names now and you better show you know this. Let's say you worked for one of these telecommunications companies that has changed names through the years, a hiring manager can tell how old you are by how you list it on your resume. So let's say the company was Southern Bell and now it's AT&T, or Air Touch Communications, which is now Verizon Wireless, and so on. If you must list experience from the early '90s and your company's name changed, just put the new name. This will at least show that you're up to date on the new name and keep the resume from looking antiquated.

8. Listing An Old College Name or Degree Title- Similar to what I stated above. I went to University of Toledo, which is in Toledo, OH, which used to be called Toledo University. I majored in Business Administrative Assisting, which is no longer offered, but Business Administration is. We had very similar course requirements and electives for obtaining a business degree, but things were different back then.

Georgia Tech (Georgia Institute of Technology) changed their business degree from a B.S. in Business Management to a B.S. in Business Administration. So now instead of a BSM it's a BSBA degree. This was to keep up with the standard degree name in the job market. You see? They're keeping up with the times too. Now although the change was made in 2011, you still want to show that you're current too. Most institutions have changed from titling themselves as "college" to "University"; however, I have seen plenty of resumes where the candidate didn't bother to change it.

9. Listing Old Computer Skills- Even if there are a couple of companies out there who still use mainframe and Lotus Notes, I wouldn't advise adding this to your resume. Unless of course that particular company is requesting this skill in the job posting. Old systems, programming languages and things that most companies have moved on from should be left off. Old versions too. "V. whatever" should be noted with the latest version. PeopleSoft is now Oracle (or some still say Oracle PeopleSoft), Peachtree is now Sage 50 Accounting and so on.

10. Listing Hobbies- Now, I know most of you know better than this. However, I have seen one or two resumes this year with some interesting and non-related hobbies listed. Your fly-fishing or drag racing hobby has no place on the resume. Most younger applicants know not to do this, so add it and you'll date yourself. Gone are the days of showing how well rounded you are.

Example of a Resume That Screams…Discriminate Against Me!

William Beckansale

If this client were in the insurance industry or any other industry that requires or values more than 20 years of experience his previous resume might have been okay; although it was lacking the meat that would paint him in the best light. However, William is in the ever-changing furniture industry.

His first resume was very dated with an old email address from a service that one wonders if it's still in existence. His years of experience were listed at the top and his job history went back too far.

To discourage any possible age discrimination, an entirely new format was created. The resume was rewritten to tell a story with loads of accomplishments. Notice the **Before** and **After** samples.

For the **After** sample, by the time he gets to the interview, a hiring manager will not care how old he may be. They will want to snatch him up for his level of expertise! Hopefully. ☺

BEFORE:

WILLIAM BECKANSALE

15436 Glendale Avenue ▪ Raleigh, NC 27602
919-220-1111 ▪ willbeck56@aol.com

Over 25 Years of Experience in Major Markets

PROFESSIONAL HISTORY

HAMILTON FURNITURE, Raleigh, NC   2011– Present
VP OF MARKETING

- Manage up to 175 individuals for 5 stores. Manage day-to-day operations, go over marketing plans and goals with managers, sales associates and technical teams. Responsible for customer experience.

Hamilton Furniture, Raleigh, NC   2011 – 2013
Regional Sales and Marketing Director

- In charge of the Southeast region, which includes GA, FL, the Carolinas, MS, AL and TN. Managed day-to-day operations, created sales plans and monitored field sales representatives for key accounts. Set goals, held training presentations and demonstrations. Found new business and sales opportunities.

Turner Furniture, Tallahassee, FL   2007 – 2011
General Manager of Sales

- Responsible for all sales and profits, human resources, training, scheduling, inventory management, ordering, vendor relationships, sales plans and customer service. Managed the busiest store in the Southeast and traveled to open up other stores as needed.
- Exceeded sales goals by 20% year-over-year.
- Received "Best in Class" award for topping other stores for sales and customer service.
- GM of the Year Award for helping the store to gain new business during all seasons.

CASE SOLUTIONS, CHARLOTTE, NC   1992 – 2007
MANUFACTURER SALES REPRESENTATIVE

- Responsible for North and Central Florida territory. Worked with furniture retailers across territory to sell products, and to gain floor placement and merchandising.

- Generated new customer base with increases from 30 to 70%.
- Led business development as a key partner of the executive team, visited customer sites.

Previous History: Seaman's: Sales Representative: 1989 – 1992 and Sales Assistant: Shemi Interiors: 1985 – 1989

EDUCATION

FRANKLIN COLLEGE GEORGIA, MAJORED IN BUSINESS MANAGEMENT: 1992 – 1995

PROFESSIONAL AFFILIATIONS
RALEIGH CHAMBER OF COMMERCE: BOARD MEMBER– Current
DURHAM CHAMBER OF COMMERCE – Former Member

AFTER:

WILLIAM BECKANSALE

15436 Glendale Ave. ▪ Raleigh, NC 27602 ▪ 919-220-1111 ▪ wb919@gmail.com

Deep-Seated Experience in Penetrating Major Markets
Action-oriented, senior-executive with a stellar career in the furniture industry. Highly respected for bringing true vision and culture to an organization. Recognized as an affirmative change agent, with proven success in leading some of the largest brands in the U.S.

Strategic- Experienced in developing business strategies that counter the competition. "Featured in Furniture Today" in 2017.

Turnaround and Growth- Successfully turned around several retailers, and delivered unprecedented growth.

Sales & Marketing- Captured a new Florida market and raised overall company sales for Hamilton Furniture; contributed to $32 million annually.

Areas of Expertise
✓ Operations Management
✓ Profit and Loss Management
✓ Market Positioning
✓ Branding Strategies
✓ Risk Assessment
✓ Consumer/Market Trends
✓ Business Development
✓ Partnership Building
✓ Training and Development

PROFESSIONAL EXPERIENCE

HAMILTON FURNITURE, Raleigh, NC   2011– Present
VP of Sales & Marketing: 2013 – Present
Originally brought on board to expand a newly developed territory in FL. Fast-tracked to current senior role managing 175 direct and in-direct reports. Direct all planning, budgeting, forecasting, and the digital customer experience.

- Conceptualized new marketing campaign for Suite Comfort line that penetrated a competitive market.
- Launched large-scale PR campaign that gained exposure in a new affluent market in Coral Gables.
- Partnered with Brand Ambassador and secured several celebrity endorsements through media events.
- Piloted an aggressive marketing plan that delivered a 21% increase in market share in West Florida.
- Secured 35 new accounts over a three-year period and raised annual revenue to over $11 million.

Continued On Next Page…

WILLIAM BECKANSALE

PROFESSIONAL EXPERIENCE

Regional Sales and Marketing Director   2011 – 2013

Recruited to lead the FL region and later took over the entire Southeast region. Developed sales plans for 20 sales representatives. Led training presentations on visual merchandising and product promotions.

- Increased luxury category sales throughout TN and AL during the first year in position.
- Drove traffic growth by 15% and grew quarterly sales by 20% in GA, NC and SC.
- Developed a new training process resulting in sales representatives being promoted to management.

TURNER FURNITURE, Tallahassee, FL   2007 – 2011
General Manager of Sales

Oversaw daily store operations for one of the busiest stores in the SE. Established all sales goals, led recruiting and hiring. Managed $15.5 million worth of inventory.

- Revitalized sales during the recession; ultimately exceeded revenue goals by 20% YOY.
- Received "Best in Class" award for ranking above other stores for sales and customer service.
- Earned GM of the Year Award for continuously driving new business during all seasons.

EDUCATION

UNIVERSITY OF GEORGIA, ATHENS
Majored in Business Management
Board Member: Raleigh Chamber of Commerce

Chapter 12

You're Transitioning With No Experience in Your Targeted Industry

Again, Why Should We Hire You Now?

You figure you're still a good fit because you recently obtained your degree. Or not... You've been eager to go into healthcare, marketing, finance, human resources or any other field that requires you to have a related degree or certification, and one to two years of experience. What are you going to put on your resume? you ask. First, you can start with your transferable skills as I mentioned in Chapter 3 and Chapter 8. Add these right in the summary or your core competencies section, where the bulk of your keywords should be. Next, I've done the following for plenty of clients and it works out for them just fine. So here ya go!

If you recently earned your degree- this is one of those times where you would list your education on the first page of the resume and your related major courses. If you have enough room, add any mock projects you've completed, whether they're group or individual, and list the grade. If the posting again has a degree as a must have...see the first solution below.

If you didn't get a degree in the field you're transitioning to, but maybe you earned a certification and have some other related professional training, add it towards the top of the resume. You can simply say, "Certified in..."

If you've joined a professional organization that's related to the new field, definitely add this. You can add this at the end of the resume as you normally would.

Now, those are things you can list to show how well you did in your studies and how immersed you are in the field already. The following pages show three examples of how to create a transitional resume.

Clayton Stone – Transitional Resume

This is a candidate who had a stellar career in banking and finance. After his bank closed down, he decided to pursue a career in Massage Therapy. The only real experience was his hands-on experience from his clinical rotations. Notice how the emphasis is on his education, customer service and sales experience.

CLAYTON STONE

clll@stonelastname.com

2631 New Road Way NW ▪ Marietta, GA 30064 ▪ 404-555-1000

CLINICAL MASSAGE THERAPIST

Certified in Natural Healing

Well Versed in: Sports & Swedish Massages, Various Products and Treatments Such as:
Reflexology, Deep Treatments, Hot Stone Therapy and Body Wraps

Profile

- Service-oriented professional committed to nurturing the development of a wellness lifestyle.
- Previous background in customer service from working in the banking and finance industry.
- Built a firm foundation in massage therapy as a graduate of Georgia Massage School.

MASSAGE THERAPY CLINICAL ROTATIONS

THE NATURAL HEALER, Atlanta, GA   April 2018 – May 2019

Gained invaluable experience by assisting 30 therapists with 6 to 8 clients per day. Included muscle treatments, encouraging healthy healing. Increased range of motion and body balance.

- Developed loyal customer base within 4 months; with a strong repeat and referral record.
- Delivered tremendous relief through deep tissue, towel massages, and hot stone therapy.
- Thoroughly documented clients' visits and followed up within two days on average.
- Received several four-star online reviews, which helped the company to be a leader in the market.

DR. CHAR MEDICAL MASSAGE, Atlanta, GA   Jan. 2018 – April 2018

Provided medical massage therapy to help clients resolve specific conditions diagnosed by Dr. Char.

- Quickly mastered the spa's state-of-the-art machines resulting in the ability to serve more clients.
- Used strong interpersonal skills to create a soothing and relaxing environment for 10 clients per day.

--Continued on Next Page--

CLAYTON STONE

EDUCATION SABBATICAL

ATLANTA MASSAGE SCHOOL, Alpharetta, GA   May 2016 – August 2018
Student
- Took the opportunity to go back to school for a transition into the massage therapy industry.
- Selected three electives in Advanced Nutrition, Rehabilitation and Neuromuscular Therapy along with core course in Humanities and Social Sciences.
- Ranked among the top students at school and one of the first to start clinical rotations.

BANKING & FINANCE EXPERIENCE

NEW CALDWELL BANK OF THE SOUTHEAST, Atlanta, GA   Feb. 2009 – May 2016
Banker/Relationship Manager
- Developed a solid customer base throughout career with a loyal consumer following.
- Led grand openings to introduce the bank and bring awareness to new communities.
- Played a key role in establishing East Atlanta branch and increased profitability from $3 to $15 million.
- Boosted profitability by $10 million for a challenging Roswell branch within 6 months.
- Launched new investment campaigns, developed new business and surpassed branch sales goals.

EDUCATION

CLAYTON COUNTY SCHOOL OF MASSAGE | Morrow, GA

Certificate of Clinical Massage Therapy: Aug. 2018

VOLUNTEERISM

Massage Therapy Foundation: Volunteer Therapist, 2017 – Present

Habitat for Humanity: Volunteer, 2016- 2018

Grace Hospice: Fundraiser, 2018

Lauren Bercliff, RN

After feeling burned out from her regular nursing duties, this candidate wanted to continue her passion in the profession, but in a different capacity—a transition to Patient or Nurse Case Management. Her resume had a job hopper's appearance as well. Most would assume she was a traveling nurse, however, just to put more emphasis on her transferable skills, a showcase format vs. a chronological one would make her more marketable instead of repetitive descriptions for all positions.

LAUREN BERCLIFF, RN

2333 Kendall Ave. | Nashville, TN 37143 | 615-222-1111 | laurenrn@outlookemail.com

VALUE OFFERED TO YOUR ORGANIZATION

Licensed Registered Nurse with a strong clinical background; poised to transition to Patient Case Management and serve as a reliable source of knowledge for continuous care and treatment. Exceptional interpersonal, written and verbal communication as well as documentation skills. **Expertise and knowledge in the following:**

Trauma | Critical Care | Long-Term Care | Neurosurgical | Cardiac Surgical ICU Consulting | Medical Claims | Patient Care Plans | Triage | Patient & Family Consulting Planning and Facilitation | ICD-9/10, CPT Coding | Writing Medical Summaries

PROFESSIONAL EXPERIENCE

Nursing-Surgical ICU/Trauma Care

- Specialize in patients with high morbidity/mortality rates, multi-system failure and hemodynamic instability. Utilize skills in IV therapy/phlebotomy, telemetry, defibrillation and cardioversion.
- Served on the emergency response and resuscitation teams. Provided intensive care to numerous patients who suffered from serious and life-threatening physical injuries.
- Managed the most complex incidents, assessed and treated within a short time frame.

Charge Nurse ~ Intensive Care Unit

- Directed daily operations and instruction for 5 to 10 staff nurses in an 18-bed intensive care unit.
- Provided a high level of patient care and exercised sound decision making skills and flexibility.
- Created Fact Sheet for nurses, a guide for cardiac medications, treatment of shock and interpretation of blood gases. Designed brochures related to the ICU for families and patients.
- Served as a Preceptor for new graduates and interns for three-month periods. Provided effective training, which led to full-time nursing positions.

EMPLOYMENT HISTORY

WELLCARE	Nashville, TN	Registered Nurse	2015 – Present
WAKE COUNTY MEMORIAL	Raleigh, NC	Charge Nurse-ICU	2013 – 2015

LAUREN BERCLIFF, RN

PREVIOUS CONTRACTOR POSITIONS

MCTA Medical	Washington, DC	Registered Nurse	2014 – 2015
NORTHEAST MEDICAL	Syracuse, NY	Charge Nurse-ICU	2013 – 2014
Grace Home Health Care	Nashville, TN	Surgical Intensive Care Nurse	2010 – 2012
Carrollton Hospital	Various TN Locations	Care Relief Nurse	2008 – 2010

EDUCATION /CERTIFICATIONS /LICENSURE

Vanderbilt University | Bachelor of Science in Nursing: 2008

Critical Care; Basic Cardiac Life Support Instructor

Active License: Tennessee #22235

Member of:

American Academy of Nursing-AAN

Jordan Michaels

Jordan started his career in human resources. Since he had a difficult time advancing from a generalist role, he decided to go back to school. By the time he finished his degree, he was already excelling in customer service. When the opportunity presented itself, he decided to transition back to human resources.

This is a transitional resume, again in a showcase format to highlight his related experience. This format is best to bring his HR experience to the forefront. Since his HR experience was so many years ago, it would most likely end up towards the bottom of the second page. A hiring manager may not make it that far.

Notice how there is heavy emphasis on his current customer service and relevant transferable experience.

JORDAN MICHAELS

57 West Park Ave. | New York, NY 10021 | 212-444-4440 | jomichal01@gmail.com

Career Focus:
HUMAN RESOURCE MANAGEMENT

Excellence in:
Business Partner Relationships, Recognizing Employee Talent and Performance Management

- ➲ Multitalented visionary leader with a vast array of career accomplishments. Well-versed in all areas of Human Resources from administration and generalist duties to implementing and managing strategic processes that create organizational effectiveness.

- ➲ Highly organized with the ability to handle multiple priorities in a matrix organization. Utilize a service/customer-oriented approach with strong interpersonal and communication skills.

- ➲ A champion of a culture that fosters diversity of thought, innovation and inclusion of all employees.

KEY COMPETENCIES

Recruiting, Hiring & Retention | Training & Development | Performance Management
New-Hire Orientation & Onboarding | Benefits & Compensation | Strategic Planning
Budget Management | HR Policies & Legal Compliance | Employee Relations

HIGHLIGHTS OF CAREER EXPERIENCE

Allstate Insurance Companies: 2006 – Present

Human Resources Administration/Recruiting

- On-boarded as a Human Resources Generalist managing day-to-day HR operations, administration of policies and procedures during Allstate's fast growth in claims.
- Developed robust relationships with HR business partners through collaboration.
- Implemented targeted recruiting strategies to address hiring needs. Focused on labor market conditions and organizational goals.
- Coached hiring managers on the talent selection process, steered negotiations and closed offers for employment.
- Instrumental in identifying top talent and matching suitable candidates for recruiters.

--Continued on Next Page--

JORDAN MICHAELS   PAGE TWO

Workforce Development, Training & Coaching

- Currently guide a team of 11 direct reports in the Enterprise Shared Services division.
- Played a key role in the advancement of 25% of the workforce being promoted.
- Turned around three underperformers to meeting and exceeding expectations through constant coaching, guidance and teamwork.
- Led 75% of the team to complete Excellence in Operations Management certificates.
- Designed an alternative work arrangement program for the entire Claims department to ensure adequate coverage while maintaining labor costs.
- Slashed the department budget by two and a half percent by collaborating with supervisor peers to identify unnecessary spending, excessive labor costs, employee performance, merits and job grades. Delivered reports to HR director as well.

Supervisory/Customer Service

- Currently lead a team of supervisors who oversee reps for complex claims and customer care center claims. Includes property, bodily injury claims and suits.
- Oversaw 35 Contact Center Representatives (remotely) for a busy call center division.
- Implemented department policies and significantly improved underperforming areas.
- Assisted in piloting and implementing a nationwide metrics platform, resulting in more real time metrics to address customer and service issues immediately.

CHRONOLOGY OF EMPLOYMENT HISTORY

Allstate Insurance Companies

Shared Services Quality Supervisor	2015 – Present
Contact Center Supervisor	2012 – 2015
Claims Representative	2009 – 2012
Human Resources Generalist	2006 – 2009

EDUCATION

Bachelor of Business Administration: 2012
State University of New York (SUNY)

CERTIFICATIONS

Human Resources Management Certificate
Organizational Leadership

PROFESSIONAL MEMBERSHIP ORGANIZATION

Society for Human Resource Management: SHRM

When trying to break into a new field, there are a number of things you can do to actually get the experience, whether paid or not. Some of these are

1. Volunteer at a non-profit agency. Non-profits need people for all sorts of tasks, from recruiting to marketing, technical support, administrative tasks and so much more.

2. If you want something in healthcare, highlight your training and clinical rotations.

3. Create a business! Become self-employed or have a side hustle. Be careful how you list this on your resume though. Don't brag too much. Rather than say Business Owner or CEO, titling yourself as an Independent Contractor or Freelancer is better. It won't raise suspicion as to whether or not you'll leave the company if you start doing well on your own. There are other reasons you want to be cautious about how you list your title when you're self-employed, but that's also for another book. Stay tuned.

4. If you prefer not to become self-employed, help some friends or neighbors out. For example, if you have a friend who has a new startup company, help them with marketing. Trying to get into information technology (IT)? Fix your friend's computer. Trying to get into an investment firm? Start trading on your own. I know several people who do this, and they say it's a full-time job.

5 . Ask a department manager within the company you work for if you can do some shadowing with the employees. And ask them for their advice on additional training or professional development courses you should take. That's what I did to get into IT and it worked!

6 . Take on some special projects on the job that are related to what you're transitioning into.

7. Join a Meetup group or two. If you're not familiar with this, it's different from the industry-related professional organizations that require an annual membership fee. They have different chapters, and so on. Meetup started around 2002. It's an online social networking portal that arranges meetings among groups. Anyone can start a group and they're just about all over the U.S. and abroad now. The majority of the groups are for socializing, traveling, dining out, seeking adventures and just about anything you can think of. Lately, a ton of Meetup groups have been established just for professionals and people specializing in certain fields. From MBAs to women in IT networking, to small business owners and the like.

You can join one of these groups for usually little or nothing (some charge dues, others charge according to the event or both). You can choose from small groups to large ones. If nothing else, it's a great way to network and learn more about who's hiring for what, when, where and how to get into a field.

8. Join your Chamber of Commerce. If you think your local chamber is for business owners and well-known corporations or politicians, think again. I have seen people who recently relocated from another city, who are trying to find a job, come to our meetings. You don't have to be a member and many events and meetings are free, such as the meet and greet and networking nights. I remember inviting one of our new clients who had just relocated from Nashville and it resulted in her getting her first job in the city. So don't be shy. Get out there and network!

Chapter 13

Using the Same Resume for Every Job You Apply for

"I am almost positive I saw this same resume for my HR Generalist position. Now they're applying for the Marine Biologist role? Get outta here!"

One of the first questions we ask a client during their initial consultation is,

"Have you seen any job postings of interest?" The next question we ask is:

"Do you meet all of the qualifications?" Many people reply:

"Well, I wanted to get my resume written first."

The fact of the matter is you need to tailor your resume to the job posting, or similar job postings of interest for your resume to be most effective. Years ago this was only a requirement for Federal Government resumes, but today it's applying more and more to traditional resumes as well. So it's pretty similar to what I mentioned in Chapter 3 (Do You Have a Job Target?).

For every client who has a great resume and tells me they haven't had any luck in getting much response or zero response, the #1 reason is usually because they're not re-tailoring and changing their resume for the next job they're applying for… or the next one after that. And trust me, I know it's a pain, but it's one of those necessary evils, so to speak. Most times you don't have to do much to change it. Just tweak it here and there. Change the summary and related keywords a bit. If necessary add more bullet points of experience to speak to whatever the job posting requires.

So don't think that all sales jobs are the same and you can use the same keywords and core competencies for the next job. Sure you may have strong negotiation skills, effective presentation skills, are able to reach C-level decision makers and so on, but many job postings require skills for specific industries. Take, for example, a medical device sales position. The posting may want you to have experience in assisting surgeons in the operating room. Do you have this experience from working in software sales? If not, then you may not want to even apply. You could, however, apply to a pharmaceutical sales rep. position because your skills would transfer over better. You still would need to re-tailor your resume to suit the qualifications. Or, what about a Registered Nurse? You may have ICU experience and the posting is asking for someone with this experience, but more specifically dealing with cardiac arrest.

Here's one of my favorites—Risk Management. This can apply to so many industries. Insurance, banking, finance, fraud, IT, healthcare, retail and many more. Some postings ask for certifications, others want experience in SOX. You have to really read these postings carefully.

If you're doing a resume blast, or simply uploading your document to every job board there is, and emailing recruiters left and right without even taking the time to tweak the wording as needed, then you're doing yourself a disservice. You could be wasting your time, and this is why you're not getting much of a response.

Chapter 14

The Career Contractor

Freelance writers, overseas contractors, PRN or travel nurses, IT professionals, skilled laborers and other professionals need a special kind of resume. If you fall into the contractor or independent category and you've been using the traditional, reverse chronological resume, you may not be putting your best foot forward and getting the results you desire. There are several kinds of resumes and/or documents that can increase your chances of a greater response. These include the following:

Contractor Resume – There are various ways to write the contractor resume. If you're contracting overseas or for a military defense company your contracts are usually for a considerable length of time. Therefore, you can use…

– Traditional/Reverse Chronological - You can create a heading that says Independent Contractor and then detail your experience. Be sure to emphasize how long the contracts were (3 months, 2 years, etc…). At the beginning of this resume or somewhere in the Experience section, be sure to list certain attributes. For example, if your contracts were overseas, you would want to highlight the fact that you can work in adverse conditions.

– Showcase Style - Remember the hybrid of a reverse chronological and functional resume I mentioned in previous chapters? Well, this is one to use if you're a contractor say... in IT healthcare training, PRN/travel nursing or something similar. You can highlight your expertise and core competencies, and then go right into the accomplishments and results you delivered to all companies, customers or clients. Using this format eliminates the need to add multiple dates throughout the year along with your role for each one. For the companies you do wish to add, you would include the names, your titles and the dates at the end.

Project Resume – After you create your summary and keywords or just a summary of keywords if you're trying to shorten the resume, list your projects or assignments in reverse chronological order. You can either detail your projects out in the traditional way, formatting them by listing the company and your title (such as Freelance Writer, Magazine Writer, Producer, Marketing Manager or the like). Remember to describe the scope of your projects and any accomplishments such as whether it was completed on time, how you overcame any obstacles, how many team members you led and anything else you can think of that would make you stand out.

Business Resume – We're finding more and more small business owners in construction, real estate, electrical, HVAC, plumbing and a host of other professions dealing with residential or commercial customers that need resumes these days. They use them for bank loans, to get investors or clients. The format should be more entrepreneurial versus employee. You want to get across to the next client or contracting company that you're the best (or one of the best) in your industry. Convince them of why they should do business with you. Remember when I said don't list over 10 years, date yourself and all that? Well with a business resume you can ignore those rules because they don't apply to you.

For a business resume you not only want to start off with your many years of experience if you're a seasoned pro, but you will want to list all of your years even if they do go as far back as the '80s because the more experience, the more trustworthy you are in the eyes of your potential client (that is provided you don't have any bad ratings with the Better Business Bureau). By the way, if you have a good rating, list that along with your other certifications.

I would recommend listing your licenses and certifications either at the beginning or end, depending on how many you have. You still want to quickly get to the point and show the specific clients you've worked with, how you helped to make their lives better, improve their business, and so on. You can also add a project list at the end. Use it as an addendum to the business resume. If your resume is sales driven, such as real estate, then you can show all of the properties you sold at the end in a list. Or if you haven't been in the industry long, just show your experience in the traditional reverse chronological order, while keeping the entrepreneurial tone.

Check out the contractor, project manager and business resume on the following pages.

Mia Carson

This candidate—an Epic healthcare software trainer was tired of contract work and wanted a permanent position, or at least one that did not require a lot of travel. Using a chronological/showcase format, again it was best due to the multitude of contract positions where she repeatedly held the same roles. Notice, this resume is three pages. We normally try not to go over two, but it is not uncommon for an IT resume (in this case IT Healthcare) to go to three pages. It's the content that matters most.

MIA CARSON

3334 Grand Mile Rd. ☐ Ann Arbor, MI 48103 ☐ (734) 474-5555 ☐ miacars@outlook.net

EPIC TRAINER

Healthcare IT Implementation

10 Years' Experience Using Epic

Proficient in electronic healthcare medical record implementation, supporting conversions. Well versed in providing elbow support for physicians, nurses and ancillary staff.

Demonstrated success in inpatient and ambulatory settings. Developed skills through in-depth training on various modules and on-site Go-Live activations.

Experienced in Epic, Cerner, MEDITECH and Allscripts. Resourceful team player and exceptional problem Solver with strong analytical skills. Known as an effective communicator able to convey complex information verbally and in writing.

CORE COMPETENCIES

Software Implementation | Project Life-Cycle | Go-Live Support | System Analysis
Physician/Assistants Support | Business Process & Procedures | IT Technical Support
Technical Skills:
EPIC Super User: Inpatient/Order Modules | Cadence | Prelude | HIM | Ambulatory
Radiant ATE Support | Revenue Cycle Systems | Microsoft Word and PowerPoint

HIGHLIGHTS OF PROFESSIONAL EXPERIENCE

Implementation/Consulting | 2015 – Present

Recruited as an Implementation Consultant for contract assignments at the following hospitals:

Kennedy Memorial Hospital-New York, NY

- Served as Team Lead for clinical workflows. Provided training, implementation and supported Allscripts Enterprise EHR.
- Provided telephone help-desk support, troubleshooting, triage for Allscripts TouchWorks and ensured all tickets were handled expeditiously.

Page 1 of 3

MIA CARSON   miacars@outlook.net

Piedmont Health System-Charlotte, NC

- Epic Ambulatory Consultant- Provided elbow support to clinical staff and providers. Included operational process behaviors as part of the go-live procedure for CPOE, ROS, Meds reconciliations and workflows.
- Assisted physicians and nurses with questions and procedures related to their Epic system.
- Guided providers and clinical staff on creating smart phrases and macros.

Northeast Memorial Hospital-Philadelphia, PA

- Epic ADT Consultant- Supported ADT and Cadence on go-live activation.
- Established close working relationships with several unit secretaries and nurses in the Cardiology department to analyze and resolve issues and problems.

Memorial Healthcare System-Tampa, FL

- Served as an Epic Inpatient Consultant. Provided Clindoc and Beacon ATE support to clinical staff, providers and HUCs during go-live implementations.
- Assisted providers with creating templates using smart phrases and by implementing smart texts.
- Provided ATE support to providers in the completion of progress notes using Dragon.
- Established a close working relationship with nurses and physicians in the Oncology department and analyzed issues.

Medical College of Ohio-Toledo, OH

- Successful in delivering Epic support to nurses, practitioners, physicians and physician assistants during Go-Live.
- Served as Epic Ambulatory Application System Analyst; provided Dragon support in addition to:
  - Epic Inpatient/Orders modules
  - Gained CPO/CPOM experience

CHRONOLOGY OF CONTRACT WORK HISTORY

Kennedy Memorial Hospital, New York, NY   Sept. 2015 – Present
Team Lead

MIA CARSON

miacars@outlook.net

CONTRACT WORK HISTORY CONTINUED

Piedmont Health System, Charlotte, NC
Ambulatory Consultant

Aug. 2012 – Sept. 2015

Northeast Memorial Hospital, Philadelphia, PA
Epic ADT Consultant

Jan. 2008 – Feb. 2012

Memorial Healthcare System, Tampa, FL
Epic Ambulatory Consultant

July 2007 – Dec. 2007

Medical College of Ohio, Toledo
Epic Ambulatory Consultant

July 2006 – July 2007

EDUCATION

Temple University, Philadelphia, PA

Bachelor of Science in Computer Engineering: 2010

CERTIFICATIONS

Epic: ASAP-Emergency Room

EpicCare Ambulatory/Inpatient: Clinical Documentation

Page 3 of 3

Kyla Sullivan

Kyla has been in project management for many years, however we only concentrated on her last 10-12 years. She chose to stay in her beloved industry, and each of her projects needed to be detailed, so there was no need to do a showcase format for her. This resume sample is in the usual chronological format. Notice she also has no degree. This is a candidate who has been progressing in her career based solely on her years of experience and success.

KYLA SULLIVAN
33 Dry Spring CT | Atlanta, GA 30304 | 404-444-4441 | kysul@comcast.net

SENIOR IT MANAGER

Proven Success in Leading Large, Multimillion-Dollar End-to-End
Data Center Infrastructure Projects
Certified as: Data Center Manager, ScrumMaster and Project Manager; ITIL Certification

CAREER HIGHLIGHTS

✓ Seasoned professional with an impeccable list of accomplishments spanning over the last 12 years. Includes directing teams in 24/7/365 mission-critical information technology environments, disaster recovery, business continuity, decommissions and data center consolidations.
✓ An excellent communicator with strong listening and interpersonal skills. Proven history of success in writing/developing continuous improvement processes and plans to drive operational efficiency.
✓ Ensured multiple concurrent IT infrastructure projects were delivered on-time, on-budget, and produced measurable business results.
✓ Successful as a change agent and mentor to as many as 50 direct reports, matrix resources and project leaders both internationally and domestically.

AREAS OF EXPERTISE

✓ Global Infrastructure Projects	✓ Planning & Implementation	✓ Clarity Service Now
✓ Data Center Migration	✓ IT Governance (ISO, SOX)	✓ Contract Management
✓ Cloud Amazon Web Services	✓ Project Management (PMO)	✓ Vendor Management

PROFESSIONAL EXPERIENCE AND ACCOMPLISHMENTS

GE Capital IT Solutions | Atlanta, GA   04/2015 – Present
Senior Infrastructure Project Manager
✓ Data Center Migrations | Applications | Core Network | Data Centers | AWS Cloud
✓ Manage a matrix Global data center environment and infrastructure projects for multiple data centers including server rebuilds, deployment, Cloud (AWS), application migrations, virtualization, asset management, service delivery, work orders and change management.
✓ Steer global IT operations infrastructure planning and support processes such as operational readiness, root cause analysis and lessons learned.
✓ Work with project teams to understand requirements interacting with development teams, product managers, along with security and application engineers. Utilize Waterfall and Agile methods.

--Continued on Next Page--

134

KYLA SULLIVAN | PAGE TWO

PROFESSIONAL EXPERIENCE CONTINUED

Key Contributions

- ✓ Formulated a framework for project manager PMO.
- ✓ Piloted Clarity Tool process at the start of position to track labor, resources, budgets and milestones.
- ✓ Praised by management for successfully completing all projects under budget.

Tech Mahindra (GE) | New York, NY | Atlanta, GA   02/2012 – 3/2015
IT Sr. Program/Project Infrastructure Delivery Manager
- ✓ Served as the liaison between Tech Mahindra, the IT outsourcing company and GE for their new data center. Managed infrastructure projects and 24/7 support operations.
- ✓ Controlled end-to-end delivery of multiple, enterprise-wide strategic initiatives throughout the project life-cycle and delivery of projects.

Key Contributions

- ✓ Strategically led vendor management and procurement. Negotiated SOW and contractual SLA's.
- ✓ Gained a complete buy-in of the team and support of the vision by showing data center, plans and goals.
- ✓ Streamlined processes, monitored the teams' progress and implemented risk trackers to minimize issues.
- ✓ Thoroughly reviewed contracts and determined what to terminate or move during the transition.
- ✓ Completed project audit, made a complete checklist of all systems/applications to ensure all ran smoothly.

ADDITIONAL DATA CENTER/PROJECT MANAGER/PROGRAM MANAGER ROLES

Intermedia Group (AT&T Contract) | Atlanta, GA   01/2009 – 01/2012
Infrastructure Technology Senior Project/Program Manager
- ✓ Piloted a $1 billion initiative to remove and replace all of SPC's, AT&T's and the former Bell South's legacy systems. Charged with the setup, strategic planning, processes and project execution.
- ✓ Established new footprint in the existing data center, which included the following:
  - Upgraded hardware/server from Unix to Linux, replaced end-of-life applications, implemented cloud services and virtualization.
- ✓ Managed up to 20 projects. Assumed additional responsibilities due to a reduction in team members.

KYLA SULLIVAN

PROFESSIONAL EXPERIENCE CONTINUED

Hewlett Packard | Atlanta, GA   07/2007 – 11/2008

Senior Data Center Deployment Manager
Infrastructure Projects and Applications for Data Centers Totaling 50,000 sq. ft.
- ✓ Led data center consolidation and migration project for new data center. Oversaw and planned new construction phase. Spearheaded all data center hardware moves and application go-live dates. Implemented policies and procedures.
- ✓ Implemented and supported high availability application architecture across all HPIT/hosted data centers.
- ✓ Ensured asset locations utilizing RFID and Altiris for 4000 servers accuracy, location and delivery status, which included detailed reporting.
- ✓ Conducted regular service reviews, managed and audited performance relative to service levels.

CERTIFICATIONS

- ✓ Certified Data Center Manager
- ✓ Certified Business Relationship Manager
- ✓ ITIL Certification
- ✓ Certified Scrum Master
- ✓ Certificate of Project Management-Georgia State University Office of Executive Programs

ADDITIONAL TECHNICAL EXPERTISE

Cisco Network | Oracle/SQL | Microsoft Office Suite, Including Project | Voice and Data Cloud Technology

Mario Ocasio

This is a business resume for a client who wanted to expand his business. All he really needed was a brief history of his overall experience and credentials. We only listed some of his largest projects through the years. This proved to be very successful. Today, we see his trucks and employees all over Atlanta. His company is huge now! ☺

Mario Ocasio, Master Electrician   3500 Wayfair Lane
License# EL234452   Smyrna, GA 30081
Sean Casteel, Business Manager   Office: (678) 222-2212
Website: marioelectric.com: Cell: (404) 780-7777
www.linkedin.com/in/mario-ocasio   E-Fax: (678) 220-4440

20+ Years of Proven Success in the Electrical Industry

Commercial ~ Industrial ~ Residential
Company Established in 2001
A+ BBB Rating

Owner of Mario's Electric, a customer-oriented company promoting honesty, respect and integrity.

Bonded and insured; Binder of insurance company: Clean Street America with $3 million in general liability insurance.

Mario's Electric is a Flat Rate Company Offering the Following Services:

- Tenant Buildouts
- New & Existing Projects
- Flat Rate or Contract
- Maintenance Schedule

- Lighting
- Troubleshooting
- Panel Upgrade
- 120/240/277/480 Volts

PROFESSIONAL EXPERIENCE

Specific Projects

Georgia Power:
Cooling Tower Project, Smyrna, GA 2018
- Served as Superintendent of this $35 million project
- Successfully completed two months ahead of schedule

Natural Gas Project, Smyrna, GA 2016
- Project currently three weeks ahead of schedule
- Served as Sub-Contractor's Superintendent for this $46 million project

Tenant Buildouts:
- The American Mart, Atlanta, GA 2013 and 2014: $2 million contract
- Hartsfield-Jackson Atlanta International Airport: Led major ramp project in 2005

-- Continued On Next Page --

- Bank of America, Atlanta, GA 2003: Technician for Service and Maintenance
- Gateway Service, Dunwoody, GA 2003: Served as Foreman for an $18 million project
- The BB&T Building, Atlanta, GA 2000: $2.5 million project
- Edwards Homes: Mableton, GA1996 – 1999: Completed all wiring for new developments

CERTIFICATIONS

Hold Certificates in the Following:

Motor Controls	2016
Foreman Training	2016
Grounding	2015
Planning and Scheduling/Labor Relations	2015
OSHA Training-Refresher	2000

EDUCATION

Bachelor of Business Administration: Georgia Southern University   2005

Other Kinds of Resumes Continued:

- **Portfolio -** No matter the industry, from marketing to graphic design or any occupation where you've completed or been involved in a myriad of projects, these deserve to be put in their own collection. This improves your resume as well and shows proof of what you described and detailed earlier. You can carry this with you, or create a website with your portfolio.

- **Resume Business Card -** This is another marketing piece that's become popular these days. List your contact information along with industry and what your areas of expertise are. You can even list a few details on the back as well. Use a headshot of yourself as your logo on the card to make a memorable impression.

SECTION III

Resume Delivery Methods

The next chapter starts off with other reasons why your resume isn't working, followed by unique or popular trends for delivering your resume.

Chapter 15

The ATS Applicant Tracking System

Are You Delivering Your Resume the Right or Wrong Way?

"What are all these characters and garbage text?
Did he just drop the f-bomb in this? In the trash it goes!"

I conducted a resume workshop for a major healthcare corporation. Prior to the workshop the coordinator and I went over the specifics for tailoring it to the employees' specific needs. I found that most of these employees knew quite a bit about how to *write* a resume, but how to *distribute* it the right way was another story. Most had never heard of the Applicant Tracking System (ATS). The employees who had heard of it, knew what it was, but didn't know there's a trick to actually getting their resume through the system. Well there is and if you don't do it right, your resume may end up with the more than 70% of candidates' resumes that go unnoticed every day.

As mentioned in Chapter 5, Are You Using The Right Keywords? an ATS system is what most companies use now to wade through the thousands of resumes submitted. This is also the easiest and quickest way to track candidates. For those of you whose companies use Customer Relationship Management (CRM) systems, it's pretty similar. More specifically, it searches for keywords and other information to find the best matches for posted jobs.

Think of it as Google for Job Searches. Such as when you search Google for something like the closest mall in Jacksonville, FL. Maybe you go a step further and add the zip code or other specifics, such as strip mall. Well, ATS systems are the same way. Available job postings are loaded into the software system. Many are designed to automatically eliminate you if you don't meet the minimum qualifications. Whether you are applying externally or internally, this is usually the first step your resume goes through before an actual human reviews it.

So let's start with the wrong way of delivering your resume through the ATS system. You've spent hours on your nicely crafted resume with a strong summary, the right keywords, accomplishments, certifications, degrees and basically all the bells and whistles that market you as a pro. You even dressed it up with shading, the right bullet points and graphics if you're in a design or sales field. You have your resume as both a PDF and Word document. You're all set and ready to go. You post your resume to one or two of the popular employment websites or job boards.

The first thing you notice when you upload or copy and paste your nice work of art is the text scatters. Remember Rob in the Introduction of this book? He was just uploading his resume without paying any attention to this. And what are those crazy symbols that you know shouldn't be on there? Instead of your dates reading as: 2012 – Present, it says: 2012 #! Present. Or, certain punctuation has other stuff like % or something else crazy like a strange looking bullet point.

You sit there and fix it. It could take you about 30 to 60 minutes. Sometimes, depending on which board you posted your resume on, you may not even know if it posted correctly or not; therefore, you never even see the crazy symbols that snuck in there. You just assume it posted okay because you didn't get an error message. Note: *You will rarely get an error message unless you just left some necessary fields blank.* What's wrong? Well the problem is the search engines, ATS systems, resume parsing and so on (all the same thing) can't interpret the text correctly.

It doesn't recognize things such as:
- **Fancy Bullet Points**
- **Shading**
- **Certain Dashes (long ones)**

- ➢ **Semi-colons**
- ➢ **Special Headings**
- ➢ **Non-Specific Keywords**
- ➢ **Keyword Stuffing**
- ➢ **Tables and Text Boxes**
- ➢ **Templates**
- ➢ **Objective Statements**
- ➢ **Lengthy Summaries (break it up)**
- ➢ **Credentials Next to Your Name**
- ➢ **Headers and Footers**
- ➢ **Abbreviations and Acronyms**

So what's the right way to make your resume play nicely with the ATS? Reformat it as an electronic or E-Resume. It's as simple as that. However, it will also take you those 30 to 60 minutes. But… you only have to do this once versus every single time you upload your resume. You'll find that most resume posting boards will list a few different formats they'll accept your resume in, which includes: American Standard Code for Information Interchange (ASCII), Plain Word Text, Rich Text Format (RTF) and for education job portals, most accept Portable Document Format (PDF). What they don't tell you is *how* to create your resume in these formats. You may think for RTF you can just save it as such, like you do for PDF. And you can; however, there are some other things you need to do as well prior to posting.

Most of the time you'll use a Plain Word Text format for uploading or copying and pasting your resume; however, I'll go over how to create an ASCII and then Plain Word Text because there are times when you'll need one or the other. Here's what you need to do:

Step 1. Copy and paste your resume into Notepad if you're using a PC with Microsoft Word. *For Mac users without MS Word, use TextEdit.*

Step 2. Change any special heading titles to something plainer, or the titles you'll be applying for.

For example, instead of Highly Successful Program Manager just say Program Manager, Registered Nurse, Legal Assistant or whatever titles you'll apply for because remember, you want to mirror the keywords from job postings as much as possible. If you're unsure and doing a resume blast, then a heading as simple as "Summary" will usually work. In fact, be sure that you use standard headings for the rest of your document as well. Some people like to put headings like Chronology of Employment History, which is fine for the nicely formatted resume, but for the E- resume it should be titled Professional Experience, Experience or something similar. The rest, such as Education, Professional Training, and the usual are fine.

If you have special fonts, characters, brackets or bullets in your contact information section or anywhere in your heading, either delete these or change them to *.

So if it looks like this:

1355 Rockwell Avenue ☎ 419.244.8755 ✉ jill.adam.gh@gmail.com
Change it to:
1355 Rockwell Avenue * 419.244.8755 * jill.adam.gh@gmail.com
or better yet, just list each item on a separate line as:
1355 Rockwell Avenue
419.244.8755
jill.adam.gh@gmail.com

Also if you have a special credential after your name such as MBA, Ph.D., etc., spell this out on a separate line. Most systems today should interpret this correctly, but spell it out just in case. For employment dates, change any dashes to the word "to," this way they read as:

2012 to Present. Or, whatever your years are. You want to make sure that dash doesn't turn into some strange looking character.

Step 3. Left align all of your text from top to bottom. Each line should not go over 65 characters; otherwise, the text will wrap. For each line that has a fancy bullet, change it to a simple asterisk (*) like the one in Step 2. This is tedious and takes the most time, but you want to be sure that your resume fits correctly and neatly in the fields of the system.

An important thing to note: If you have any text boxes, headers and footers, tables, columns or anything fancy housing your core competencies or highlighted experience, when you copy and paste your resume onto Notepad, it will disappear. Just as an ATS System doesn't recognize these things, neither does Notepad. Therefore, you will need to recopy and paste that section without the shading, tables, etc... or retype that portion onto the Notepad document. This is another reason why it's best to first create your E-Resume in Notepad because it tends to eliminate certain things, reminding you to re-add them before you post your document to the resume boards.

Step 4. Now that you have the text all left aligned and the fancy stuff reformatted as well, save this and title it with your name and ASCII Text resume. You'll notice it looks rather digitized, but that's okay. It's perfectly fine for the systems to interpret.

Step 5. Create the Plain Word Text version. Copy and paste the ASCII Text resume onto a Word document. Now, you'll notice all kinds of green and red lines underneath most words if your spelling and grammar tool (spell check) is turned on. Remember Word doesn't recognize fragmented sentences. Delete these. I know, another tedious pain, but you want a clean appearance, don't you? And don't worry, this Plain Word Text version won't take nearly as long as it did to create the ASCII Text. With this version, you can also dress it up a little. For each of your headings you can either make them bold or use caps. You can also use a double ** for some of your bullet points if you want. Once finished, save it with your name and Plain Word Text Resume. All done!

For RTF and PDF formats, click **File, then Save As**

A Format list will come up at the bottom with the selections:

Word Document (.docx)

Word Template (.dotx)

Rich Text Format (.rtf)

PDF

Web Page (.htm) and some others

Select the desired format, then click Save.

See an example on the next page of how it should look. Brace yourself. It's not very pretty. ☺

ANGELA SHUKER, REGISTERED NURSE
911 Clearbrook Course SW
Marietta, GA 30064
678-469-7000
ajshuker1@gmail.com

VALUE OFFERED TO YOUR ORGANIZATION

Passionate, goal-oriented management
professional focused on patient-centered
care.
Proven success in clinical and
administrative leadership roles,
facilitating daily operations,
patient flow and safe delivery of care.
Extremely task driven with strong
organizational and time management skills.
Employ effective interpersonal communication
strategies when interacting with patients,
team members and other healthcare professionals.

AREAS OF EXPERTISE

* Staff Management
* Hiring, Training and Development
* Budget Management
* Managing Labor Costs
* Operations Management
* Donor Oversight
* Quality Control/Assurance
* Safety Techniques
* Corrective and Preventative Action
* State, Federal Regulations and Compliance
* Process Improvement

PROFESSIONAL EXPERIENCE

MEDIC BioCenters, Inc.
Atlanta, GA
2008 to Present

Center Director: Marietta: 2014 to Present
Brought on board by the Vice President to
assist with startup operations of an additional
center.

Steer daily operations for a plasma collection
center assisting 800 to 1200 donors per week,
while overseeing 3 direct and 25 in-direct reports.

Manage the budget, with a focus on meeting annual
production and budget targets. Direct human
resources and production planning. Ensure regulatory
compliance, and effective staff training to support
a safe plasmapheresis process for regulatory success.

Key Contributions

*   Prepared center for the following initial audits with success:
    2014:
** FDA audit resulting in zero findings by the regulatory agency.
    Awarded a two-year certification.
** GHA audit with no 483 observations.
** 2017: audit success; awarded maximum three-year extension.
*   Implemented a new employee tardiness policy that reduced
    occurrences from 42 to 9 per week.
*   Realized a rise in plasma collections from 5 to 930 per week.

Operations Supervisor: 2012 to 2014
Selected to newly created position rewarding previous performance.
Oversaw daily operations of the Norcross donor center and 30 team
members including: RNs, LPNs, phlebotomists and medical assistants.

Key Contributions

* Led relentless drive to fully develop the position through
  effective budget management, setting up human resources
  operations, which included hiring, training and implementing
  corrective action plans for donor system issues.

Physician Substitute/Front-End Supervisor: 2008 to 2012
On-boarded as the first nurse to assist in opening new location

which quickly grew to 20 staff members.

Counseled donors on reactive test and laboratory results as well as physical examinations. Oversaw front-end staff
and led training, scheduling, disciplinary action and counseling.

Key Contributions

* Successfully completed 85% of new donor examinations in the first year of operation despite limited staffing.

* Served as an exemplary leader displaying tenacity and a positive attitude, which increased team morale.

North Atlanta Plasma, Inc.
Atlanta, GA
2004 to 2008
Nurse Manager for Medical Analysis

* Reviewed blood work, pulmonary function tests, EKGs and medical history from employee annual exams of various organizations. Trained all new nurses on the medical review process.

EDUCATION

Bachelor of Science: (BSN): May, 2019
The University of Alabama, Tuscaloosa

Associate of Science: Nursing
Georgia Perimeter College

The following page shows an example of how most resumes look (or should look) when posted to a job search engine resume board, *after* it's converted to an ATS format. This is an old resume I picked from our files, with the contact and company information changed, of course. This was posted to many job search engines. Some systems have you create a profile, then manually create your resume or upload it. Others just have you upload without creating a profile. And then there are the newer systems that don't have special fields for your text. When you upload your resume it's on your dashboard. For the companies that still do it the former way (with the fields) that's what the following example is. If you use a job portal such as this, your resume should fit neatly into the fields.

RESUME TITLE: <u>Edit</u>

Test   **Resume ID:** 88373646

RESUME STATUS <u>Edit</u>

Private - This resume is not searchable by employers.

CONTACT INFO <u>Edit</u>

James Tischini
1001 Bright Way
Peachtree City, Georgia 3000
US

E jt@icloud.com
P 000-000-0000

UPLOADED RESUME <u>Edit</u>   <u>BACK TO TOP</u>

James P. Tischini
1001 Bright Way, Peachtree City, GA 30269
Home: (678) 364-2002
Cell: (678) 571-3121
jt@icloud.com

QUALIFICATIONS

An innovative, growth-oriented IT professional with 13 years' experience
in Banking Operations. Thorough knowledge of the securities industry from
handling various projects for investment clients. A skilled problem solver
with a verifiable record of achievement in exceeding expectations.
Additional values offered include:

** Experienced in applying relevant technical knowledge in auditing
  financial statements, and performing basic analysis to identify potential
  non-compliance standards.

** Recognized as the key resource for strategically handling customer
  escalations to resolve process deficiencies, system and performance issues.

** Provide leadership in vendor negotiations pertaining to acquisition of products and services. Approve contracts associated with hardware, software, and vendor support services.

**Accustomed to managing multiple projects and lead a highly technical staff in meeting deadlines.

**Daily monitor and communicate project progress to ensure that quality measures, customer process impact, milestones, business value, and risk are met and addressed.

TECHNICAL SKILLS

Microsoft Office, MS Query, SQL, AM Trust Accounting System, SunGard Series 11/AddVantage Trust Accounting System, SEI Trust Accounting System and Securities Processing

PROFESSIONAL EXPERIENCE

2005 to Present * Reliance Trust Company
Atlanta, GA
IT Application/Project Manager

Responsible for ensuring the SunGard AddVantage Trust Accounting System functions properly. Maintain availability, system security, network connectivity, user access, system upgrades and enhancements, night processes and internal system reconciliation. Report directly to CIO.

* Key person for Security and Exchange Commission reporting.
* Sole manager for reconciling tens of millions of dollars for 13 major accounts.
* Designed and implemented a new automated processing system for Prudential Investments to facilitate reporting and trading.
* Primary leader for annual company-wide year-end tax form preparation.
* Maintain four different databases totaling 150,000 accounts worth $9 billion in market value. Insure all problem areas are covered and errors reduced.

* Create ad hoc reports using SQL interface for management, customers internal and external government auditors.
* Provide development personnel with knowledge of table structure and processes, which assist in several external applications that perform tasks unavailable within the main system.

Client Services Manager

Managed group of client relationship liaisons responsible for coordinating system training, account coding, problem resolution, accurate and timely statement and tax document production for all internal and external clients.

•Created Outsourcing Department which led to company's major profit producing area.
•Led several new customer migrations adding over $1 billion in assets under custody.
•Assisted in bringing in larger clients, increasing accounts by 100% and assets by 200%.
•Implemented a new process for customer Common Trust Fund valuation.

2000 to 2005 * Bank of America, Atlanta, GA
Operations Officer/Income Processing Supervisor

Promoted progressively from ATM Teller. Directed a team of specialists processing client income from various sources such as stocks, fixed income, mortgages and asset-backed assets ensuring timely payment and collection.

•Steered Income Area during corporate merger and area shutdown, while ensuring
  clients' high expectations of banking services and standards were always met.
•Project team member for installations and upgrades of new ATMs in all Georgia banks.

EDUCATION

Georgia State University, Atlanta
Bachelor of Business Administration: 2005

COMMUNITY ACTIVITIES

Regularly coach youth baseball and football

WORK EXPERIENCE Edit		BACK TO TOP
Dates Employed	**Job Title**	**Company**
2015 to Present	**Project Manager**	Reliance Trust
EDUCATION Add		**BACK TO TOP**

SKILLS Add   BACK TO TOP

Skill Name	Skill Level	Last Used/Experience

LANGUAGES Edit   BACK TO TOP

Languages	Proficiency Level
English	Fluent - Full Knowledge

CAREER INFO Edit   BACK TO TOP

Current Career Level:

Experienced (Non-Manager)

Years of relevant work experience:

10+ to 15 Years

Military Service:

No

Active Security Clearance:

No

TARGET JOB Edit   BACK TO TOP

Work Status:	**US** - I am authorized to work in this country for any employer.
Desired Type:	Employee, Temporary/Contract/Project

Desired Status:	Full-time
Desired Salary:	80,000.00 USD Per Year
Job Titles:	Telecommunications, Consultant
Company Size:	No Preference
Categories:	Telecommunications
Industries:	All
Locations:	US-Georgia-Atlanta North
Willing to relocate:	No

RELATED INFO Edit   BACK TO TOP

Desired Work Shifts:	First Shift (day)
Weekend Preference:	Yes
I can start	Immediately

I'm Finished

Some Do's and Don'ts to Remember:

Do remember to delete any acronyms from your E-Resume and spell out the words, including those of professional organizations, certifications and industry lingo.

Don't stuff your resume with keywords (aka keyword stuffing). Years ago people used this tactic thinking they could trick the ATS systems and scanners with all sorts of keywords that weren't even relevant, but these systems are pretty savvy now. And besides, it doesn't impress recruiters, it only irritates them.

Don't hide or whiteout your keywords thinking the systems will detect it, yet hide all the extra words from the employer. There's a myth going around where people think they can just turn the text from black to white and trick the system, loading it with a gazillion key words. This doesn't work either.

Do mention relevant keywords at least twice (or three or more times, depending on your positions) throughout your resume. Instead of listing your keywords or core competencies in a single list at the beginning of your resume, you're showing actual examples of having these skills.

Do get assistance with keywords if you must. I always suggest going with the job postings of interest, as I showed in the earlier examples. If you don't have any particular ones right now, and it's too time consuming to sift through a gazillion postings (for those who are just updating your resume for a future search), you can also find more keywords through Google or Bing search engines. Type in Ways to Find Keywords for a Resume, and a number of websites that provide resume keywords will pop up. Did you know there are even keyword *books*?

You can also ask a hiring manager for assistance. For example, if you're applying to a specific company and you have a contact person, ask them what they usually look for.

I've asked myself for several of our senior-level clients whenever the job posting was a little vague.

Chapter 16

Sending Your Resume by Email

You know the old saying *If I had a dollar for every time...?* Wait... I said that already, didn't I? Well, that's what I think of when I see a resume in my in-box copied and pasted into the body of the email incorrectly, with the text all scattered, extra characters and everything else that hurts my eyes. And I don't know if it's that people don't take the time to check their Sent folder to see how their email went through, or they are convinced it's okay because it looked fine on their end. Usually, I have to ask the person to re-send it as an attached Word document. No one has ever sounded as though they thought it looked fine before, so I don't know what's going on with that.

What I do know though, is if you send your resume the wrong way to a recruiter, he or she may not even look at it. Yep, they'll just skip it because they already have hundreds of resumes to go through. That's right, even with the ATS system doing most of the work for them. They still have to go through the ones that made the cut through the scanning system. Many times you may be invited to email your resume. This is when the ASCII Text E-Resume comes in handy. That's why I said in the previous chapter to create that first and then the Plain Word Text. It's easier to create the Plain Word text by creating the ASCII one first and again, some systems request one or the other, or both. This means you are prepared either way.

When you submit your ASCII text resume in the body of the email, you don't need to lead in with what the email is about. You know how you start it off with the person's name and some details, such as my resume is attached, please contact me once you review... Adding a quick note in the subject line with your name and resume attached will suffice.

Emailing as an attachment is the most preferred method. And make sure you attach it just as requested. If the recruiter or hiring manager requests a Word document don't send it as a

Google Doc. If they say PDF, don't send a zip file. Send the resume in whatever format they request. Not the format you choose. They may only be able to open certain documents. Another thing you can do when emailing it as an attachment is you can add a cover note or some say an e-note in the body of the email. These are similar to cover letters only they're a lot shorter. They are a great way to introduce yourself.

Now, if a hiring manager already told you to send a cover letter along with your resume as attachments, then of course there's no need to add the cover letter in the body of the email. Just let them know both are attached. This is when you can add something to the effect of "when you're available to discuss further," ask them to let you know if they don't receive it properly, etc...

Chapter 17

Uploading Your Resume to Social Media

"Don't use social media? Sure you do. Everybody does. No? You better start!"

There are a few different social media platforms you can upload your resume to. **LinkedIn,** the professional social networking site is the most widely used for this purpose. Many think this will replace the standard resume, but that couldn't be further from the truth (at least at the time of this writing). LinkedIn and any other social media network board you use to post your resume on helps, but if a recruiter takes interest, they'll more than likely want to see your actual resume. They can't print it out from the social media site. Although, I might add I've heard of several hiring managers who hired candidates right from LinkedIn without viewing a paper or E-Resume. So of course there are exceptions.

My point, though, is the purpose of LinkedIn and any other social network is to get the hiring manager to ask you for your resume. And vice versa. If you submit your resume any other way, the hiring manager will want to know if you're on LinkedIn. They don't ask if you're on Facebook or any of the others (They'll just check for themselves to see how you present yourself). Because of course if you're not on LinkedIn you don't exist (in their eyes). By the way, you can attach your resume on LinkedIn as well. Just click on the Upload Media button in the summary section. Depending on how you're conducting your search you may not want to upload it. Remember, the key is to get someone to ask to view it. However, if you do, be sure to still build out your LinkedIn profile along with the upload.

Facebook has recently become popular for posting your resume. If you're going to do so, you may want to have a separate account for professional purposes. This way, you're not inviting a hiring manager into your private space that you share with your friends and family. Create a Facebook page that talks all about your career, projects you've worked on and anything else that may not be detailed on the resume.

161

Twitter, believe it or not, is creating huge waves these days. You can describe yourself in 280 characters. That's right! It was originally called the 140-character resume, but now it's 280 characters. The Wall Street Journal has talked about it, Huffington Post and CNN have an article on it too. And they're not the only ones. There are Career Resource websites that have also spread the social media resume gospel. This has been going on for about five or six years now. When I read these articles I thought, *Hmm… we may eventually go back to the one page resume for everyone after all!*

All you do is come up with a catchy tagline and tweet it. Let's say you're a marketing professional. You could say something like: Need a Good Event Planner? I just Managed a 2000 + Event. Hire Me!

And you still have room to add your LinkedIn or other social media address.
Or…
Innovative IT Director Who Knows How To Build an Infrastructure. Contact me #Iknowsystems.

You can quickly talk about awards you've won, projects you've completed for a particular industry and so on. Who knew there was so much you could say in only 280 characters!

Now that's just the resume part, of course, but stay tuned for my next book where I talk about why your career search isn't working, and how Twitter and other social media networks can help.

Pinterest is another new avenue for job seekers. It's no longer just for sharing recipes, fashion and other lifestyle content. Now you can post your resume or visual resume and portfolios of your work. You have to have an invite, but that's easy. It works in conjunction with Twitter and Facebook, so all you need is one of those profiles to get started.

Once you get the invite then you just create, pin and share it! More specifically…

Create your board - You'll want to create a pinboard for your job search. Just add a title that you would add when posting to a job board, or you can get creative as candidates do with LinkedIn and start off with Respected Thought Leader or Top-Performing, Results-Driven or anything that makes you stand out.

Pin It - Pin your resume, additional accomplishments you want to highlight, publications, projects, awards and anything else that makes you the crème-de-la-crème! Mainly, you want to show how you're a leader in your field so this is where you can kind of brand yourself too. Add any additional interests that you wouldn't add on the traditional resume due to lack of room, such as *how* active you are in any professional organizations, speaking engagements with photos, volunteering for special causes (except anything religious or political unless you're in these arenas).

Share it - This is where you let everyone, all of your friends and followers, know when you've pinned something, of well… interest. Hence the name Pinterest. ☺ Follow up with all of your networks. For example, whenever I post an article on LinkedIn, it invites me to copy it to my other social media networks. You can do the same thing. Reach out to your Twitter followers and your Facebook friends.

There are other social networking services out there that some job boards have like Plaxo by Simply Hired. The three I mentioned are the most popular at the time of this writing. One more thing I found that you may or may not be familiar with is creating a professional blog about your work. I happened to see one when I was trying to find out more information about a client's company. I ended up coming across a blog from one of her peers. She went into detail about their internship, even mentioned my client, so I was able to get a lot of details. I told my client about it and she confirmed it. This helped a lot. Then I found that this was something else very popular.

You don't have to use all of these methods because after a couple of them, it may seem redundant adding all of the same aspects. Here's what others who are active on social media do; post on LinkedIn, then tweet the post, share a little snippet on Facebook, and then invite friends to view everything on LinkedIn. Or, try one or two of the methods I mentioned above. Whatever you do, just get your resume out there and keep it out there. Even when you're not looking, because you never know when a great opportunity will arise.

SECTION IV

Why Your Federal Resume Isn't Working

Chapter 18

You Didn't Follow the Posting Exactly

Does this USA Jobs.Gov posting look familiar to you?

Contract Specialist

LIBRARY OF CONGRESS

Agency Contact Information

2 vacancies in the following location:

Washington DC

Work Schedule is Open – Permanent

Opened Wednesday 6/1/2018 (4 day(s) ago)

Closes Thursday 6/30/2018 (25 day(s) away)

Salary Range

$77,490.00 to $100,736.00 / Per Year

Series & Grade

GS-1102-12/12

Promotion Potential

12

Supervisory Status

No

Who May Apply

Anyone may apply - By law, employment at most U.S. Government agencies, including the Library of Congress, is limited to U.S. citizens. However, non-citizens may be hired, provided that other legal requirements are met and the Library determines there are no qualified U.S. citizens available for the position.

Control Number

440670500

Job Announcement Number

160111

And then after the basic requirements such as your degree and fields of study, the actual job description looks like this:

Duties

As a contract specialist at the Library, you will have the opportunity to work with leaders in their fields to understand and help them fulfill their needs through contractual relationships. You will research and provide guidance on complex issues such as contract structure, negotiation strategies, and performance management in support of your clients' missions.

You will perform all aspects of contracting transactions, from planning, soliciting, evaluation, and recommendation of award, to procure specialized goods and services. Your portfolio may include preservation services, building services, supply and production items, architectural engineering, serial subscription services, books and library publications, information retrieval services, and training services, etc.

You will analyze requirements, recommend revisions to statements of work or specifications, milestones, evaluation criteria, reporting requirements, and other contractual terms and conditions. You will conduct research to identify sources...

And it just goes on for about another three paragraphs.

Then it shows:

Qualifications

Applicants must have had progressively responsible experience and training sufficient in scope and quality to furnish them with an acceptable level of the following knowledge, skills, and abilities to perform the duties of the position and also without more than normal supervision.

Knowledge, Skills and Abilities (many postings don't have these now):

Knowledge of the Federal contracting laws, regulations, policies, and procedures.

Ability to solicit, evaluate, negotiate, award, and administer contracts.

Ability to analyze and solve problems related to contractual issues and make recommendations.

Ability to communicate in writing.

Security Clearance- Not Applicable (or it may request secret security clearance)

And this also had more KSAs.

Whew, those are long! I pared that former posting down a bit. There are other sections to that as well, but you get the gist. The thing to note here is everything that this posting says, or any other one on USA Jobs.Gov, you must meet. And you have to tailor your resume **for one specific posting.** When we create traditional resumes for our clients, we invite them to submit up to three job postings of interest. This helps us to see their interests, commonalities, keywords and such. Usually, we can tailor their resume with a little bit from each posting. Not so when it comes to the Federal Government. And they are strict! Their point system will and does add and deduct points for every item they look for. You have to "show" how you meet the qualifications of the specific posting so that the Human Resources office can "certify" your resume. They're trying to see if you have specialized experience or experience that's directly related to the job announcement. Here are a few ways the Federal resume is similar to and different from the civilian resume.

Similarities:

You still generally don't go back further than 10-15 years for experience.

You still tell a story and add accomplishments or results of your duties.

You can use one of the three usual formats: Chronological, Functional or Combination. Chronological is the most preferred format.

You still add the usual headings and sections such as Experience, Education and so on...

You can choose whether to use the brief paragraph description and then bullet points or simply all bullet points.

Differences:

The average federal government resume is **3 to 5 pages long.**

You MUST tailor your resume to the specific job posting and list the job announcement number at the top.

After your contact information you must list your complete address, telephone number and email address. None of that leaving off the address and just listing your zip code, or city and state. The Federal Government doesn't play that. I'm just saying.

You *can* list an objective without them frowning upon it. Actually, the objective is the job announcement title and number, so you still want to write it in a way that shows what you can do for the particular organization. We hardly ever use the heading Objective though. Career Focus, Summary of Qualifications or something similar looks better.

You should list your social security number (or the last 4 digits) at the top of the resume along with Veteran's Points. You'll add this on the application anyway.

You automatically get 5 points for being a veteran and 10 if you are disabled.

Add any security clearance.

For good measure, if you are a current federal employee, you can also add your highest GS level to date.

In the Experience section of your resume, for every position you must list:

Company Name and Dates of Employment

Address, City, State and Zip Code, or at least address, city and state, or country you've worked in.

Supervisor's Name, Title and Telephone Number

Your Title

Your Salary (preferably beginning and ending or current)

Hours Worked Per Week.

It should look something like this:

Internal Revenue Service   06/2004 – Present

2567 West Corolla Street $59,000 per year

Syracuse, NY 13222   40 hours per week

Manager: Karen Wisely (315) 526-XXXX

Okay to Contact

Internal Revenue Agent, GS-11

Examine tax returns of individuals and small businesses of various sizes and assess tax due penalties….

And then just finish listing your experience and follow up with bulleted accomplishments. Remember to stay relevant to the job posting.

Chapter 19

Did You Answer the KSAs, PTQs, TQs or any other Qs?

As time goes on you'll start to see these less and less as the Federal Government has mostly done away with them. I always wondered why these were necessary anyway when you're already mentioning your qualifications throughout your job descriptions. Still, for the few job postings you come across with these requirements, you must follow the process. Whether you find your ideal job posting on USA Jobs, DC Government Jobs, QuickHire, FAA or AVUE, you're bound to come across one of these lists with questions that you must answer in narrative form. Years ago your answers were required to be on separate documents because the answers would be more like an essay, with several pages. Now, you can add KSAs right on the resume and they're not as lengthy.

Knowledge, Skills and Abilities (KSAs) are usually used for management level positions and below. The Qs, as I like to call them, are usually for Senior Executive Service (SES) members. The Q acronyms and what they stand for are below:

PTQs- Professional Technical Qualifications

ECQs- Executive Core Qualifications

MTQs- Military Training Qualifications

TQs-Technical Qualifications

Have you been in situational interviews before? If so you are probably familiar with the STAR method. When answering any of these it's best to answer in First Person using this popular style because it's easier and your answers will be more concise. For those of you who don't know or need a reminder STAR is

Situation

Task

Action

Result

Here's a retail example:

Situation – Set the context for your story. For example:

"We were expected to be busy for the Christmas Eve holiday and two people called in sick."

Task – State what you were accountable for.

"As supervisor, I was responsible for handling last minute shift changes and ensuring we were adequately staffed to assist our customers."

Action – State what you did to resolve this issue.

"Remembering that there's always someone in our company in need of extra holiday cash, I called our backup list and was able to get two replacements and another one on stand-by before the holiday rush started."

Result – How did this end and what was your major contribution or success.

"All departments ran smoothly, customers were given personalized attention as necessary and the lines moved quickly. I even called our stand-by, which enabled us to assist more customers and increase our sales."

Other than the list of example KSA statements from the previous chapter, you may come across one like this: **Ability to lead and manage organizations, programs and people**

You will want to provide as many details as possible. And although each answer doesn't have to be a page long, if it's at least half a paragraph that's fine. Use the STAR method for this. If it gets lengthy and even goes to one page, not to worry because the HR department wants you to prove in the best way possible that you meet these qualifications.

Now, ECQs will usually have about five questions or points. They're usually the same ones, and you have to show examples of:

ECQ1-Leading Change

ECQ2-Leading People

ECQ3- Results Driven

ECQ4-Business Acumen

ECQ5- Building Coalitions

With the ECQs (and remember this is for SES candidates), there are also Core Competencies. Non-SES candidates would normally answer these in the beginning of the resume, but when it comes to ECQs, they should be paired together. The core competencies are usually more of your attributes or traits that include those below:

- Interpersonal Skills
- Oral Communications
- Integrity/Honesty
- Written Communication
- Continual Learning
- Public Service Motivation

When answering these, be sure to go into detail to show how you meet these qualifications. For example, Written Communication could be process manuals you've created. Oral and Written Communication could be PowerPoint presentations. Include what the processes were, how they solved a problem, tell how many people you created documents and presentations for and so on. Continuous Learning could go into your own professional training and development. Any courses you took, or certifications and licenses you obtained, be sure to elaborate in great detail. If there's anything grand to add such as finishing quicker than the normal time frame, say so.

So I guess it's actually a good thing that the Federal Government makes you jump through hoops to make it through the scanning process. It's a lot of work, but it actually helps you because between the resume, cover letter, KSAs, Core Qualifications and occupational questionnaire, you have plenty of opportunities to make yourself shine. Take and use them!

SECTION V

Last, But Not Least

Chapter 20

Add a Cover Letter

I Don't Care What They Told You

Unless… you're doing a resume blast. When you're posting to one of the national job search engines or boards, employers rarely, and I mean *very* rarely, read the cover letters. Above, I imply that you should always submit a cover letter, but see, there's always an exception. I can honestly say for our company job postings, out of the thousands of resumes I've received along with cover letters, I've only read maybe five that were actually good. So I, along with a lot of employers usually bypass them. Besides, most boards charge to view resumes, so why pay extra for cover letters that we know might be generic? It's really a waste of time since most aren't tailored to the positions posted. They include extra things we either don't care about, didn't ask about in the posting, or they're just too general and…. just sad.

On the other hand, if you're applying directly to an employer either by email or on their company website, then yes, definitely add one if it's requested. Many do invite you to send one. People usually take more time with these letters. A good cover letter alone can practically put you at the top of the pile and in the recruiter's favor. Then the resume is just to seal the deal. I've heard candidates say on plenty occasions that they were praised for their cover letter, or they believe the cover letter is what actually helped them. I know I love it when a candidate gives key important details that make them qualified, or takes the time to do a little research on our company and add why they're particularly interested in the job posting.

The cover letter should not have the exact same information that's on your resume. No need to state where you work and your title unless you're going into some details not mentioned on the resume.

Here's an example of a good cover letter. This is a young candidate who did mention former companies not mentioned on his resume. You'll notice throughout the letter he's proving in every way possible how he meets the qualifications.

Brandon Smith

4560 North Ave. ● Atlanta, GA 30308 ● (404) 234-5678 ● brandons@gmail.com

Date

Contact Name
Company
Address
City, State & Zip

Dear Mr./Ms. (or Recruiter)_____:

In today's economy, it takes a team of dedicated professionals to win prominence in the market place. Therefore, if you are seeking a highly motivated team player with a thorough understanding of how to develop strategic sales and marketing plans, then I invite you to review the attached resume for consideration.

You will find that I offer a unique blend of talents that are transferable to any marketing coordinator or representative role. My strengths lie in the ability to quickly master new processes, multitask in fast-paced environments and maintain quality customer service. I have also been highly instrumental in the following:

➢ Researching trends and analyzing data for promotional marketing purposes.
➢ Building customer relationships and increasing customer retention.
➢ Brainstorming ideas to help customers increase their sales and growth in targeted markets.
➢ Implementing customized solutions to resolve customer problems that hinder revenue goals.
➢ Developing PR campaigns to gain more exposure for growth-oriented companies.

These are just a few areas of knowledge and hands-on experience I gained while serving in a highly rewarding, six-month internship. This is in addition to serving in customer service and sales roles for CVS and Enterprise-Rent-A-Car.

I would welcome the opportunity to meet with you to discuss further, your goals and how I can assist you in achieving them. Please contact me at your earliest convenience for an interview. I look forward to meeting you and learning more about your company.

Sincerely,

Brandon Smith

Here are some quick Do's and Don'ts for the cover letter:

Do date the letter and address it to whomever is doing the recruiting. If you don't have a name and address, then Dear Recruiting Manager, Dear Hiring Manager or something similar will suffice.

Do state the title of the job posting and where you saw it.

Do list additional related qualifications that aren't mentioned on your resume.

Do show accomplishments from your previous jobs and how they relate to the position.

Do let the recruiter or hiring manager know if you're willing to travel or relocate if the posting mentions this, or if the company is national or global.

Don't make the cover letter longer than a page. If you can keep it to less than a page, that's even better.

Don't make excuses for qualifications you may not meet. You'll just undersell yourself. For example, if the posting is requiring five years of experience and you're one year shy, don't even mention it. Just talk about the qualifications you do meet. I mean, if you *insist* on applying for this position. Hey, I wouldn't just bypass a position for one year less of experience. I'd give it a try anyway. Next one...

Don't go into detail about why you left your previous job. Of course you know not to bad mouth anybody, but even saying something as innocent as you were laid off could hurt you. Whether it was a merger or acquisition, a lot of hiring managers will wonder why you weren't good enough for them to keep you.

Don't give health issues as to why you've been away from the workforce for a while either. I remember a client who used to put this in all of her letters and wondered why no one called her for an interview. It was a survival story and very touching; however, employers just saw it as a red flag. Once she stopped talking about it she started getting calls left and right!

Don't state an *all about you* objective. The fact that you may be seeking a company with opportunity for advancement, blah, blah, blah... well we *hope* you don't want to stay stagnant! The employer is thinking *what can you do for me?* So tell how you'll solve a problem and ultimately, make their job easier.

Don't provide unsolicited salary requirements. Especially if it's listed on the job posting! Trust me, I've seen this plenty of times. If it's not asked, don't tell.

Don't brag about things that are non-relevant, like being captain of the Lacrosse team in high school, or being roommates with a well-known celebrity. Nobody cares! Wait...some people are star struck.

Don't mention that you're willing to travel or relocate if it actually depends on certain circumstances, and you need to know more about the job first. Saying it just because it sounds good, well, you may regret it later.

There are lots of don'ts, huh? Well *do* them and you'll end up in the slush pile quick! Just remember, it's always good to be prepared with a cover letter because somewhere along the way a recruiter or hiring manager will want to see it. Keep a general, industry-related one handy that you only have to tweak every so often.

A Final Word on Resumes

As they say (and as you see I say it too), there are always exceptions to the rules. What works for one recruiter may not work for another. Believe it or not, some of them just aren't up-to-date with modern resumes, or they may be looking for a seat warmer. One thing that is pretty much the standard across the board, though, is they want to know what you can do for them. The bottom line is how you can help them make money, save money and save time. You do this by starting with the most effective marketing tool you can create. This is your professional resume.

I hope this book, which is the first in a series to help you in your job search, has been helpful. It's not quite over yet, though. I have some more tips on the following pages. You can always check out more on our blog at https://blueprintresumes.com. The next few pages show several resume samples. These include an elementary school teacher, some senior executives and federal government resumes to give you a complete idea of how most of these are created.

As always…

Good luck in your job search!

KATRINA CAMPBELL

4567 Oak Ridge Trail ♦ Mableton, GA 30126 ♦ (404) 944-1447 ♦ camishac@gmail.com

EXPERTISE

Pubic Speaking
Consumer Market Trends
Research & Analysis
Project Coordination
Building Relationships

PROFILE SUMMARY

MARKETING ANALYST / SPECIALIST
Detail-oriented marketing professional with proven results in the penetration of a new market area. Experienced in writing proposals, website development and participation in promotional events.

PROFESSIONAL EXPERIENCE

United Blood, Marketing Coordinator
Atlanta, GA 2009 – Present

Recruited to execute geographic market analysis and positioning for new donor location (2008).

Assist with writing proposals. Identify and implement successful promotional efforts targeting under-represented demographics

Collaborate with Blood & Marrow Transplant Group of Georgia.

Key Accomplishments

☑ Exceptional ability to identify target markets, increasing market share.
☑ Selected as key representative to present report findings at regional meetings to diverse audiences.
☑ Consistently finish projects ahead of deadline.
☑ Expanded marketplace exposure, resulting in 20% increase in donors at Marietta location.
☑ Helped realize exceptional branch growth in past six months; vying for #1 producer of donations in region.

JM Huber Corporation, Marketing Assistant
Atlanta, GA 2005 – 2007

Presented proposals and information to diverse audiences at staff conferences regarding: promotion, distribution and services.

Stimulated client sales leads, focused business relations and distributed company literature.

Demonstrated ability to adapt to situations and improve procedures.

Provided executive level support to Marketing Department with PowerPoint presentations and spreadsheets with sales forecasting.

Key Accomplishments

☑ Revamped entire process for adding company information to intranet system.
☑ Assisted with developing a new marketing budget to align with quarterly goals.
☑ Set the standard for researching new market trends that saved marketing managers 4 hours per week.
☑ Slashed freelancer costs by 30% after locating professionals through Elancer and Guru.com.
☑ Provided insight to creative team on how to target millennials and gain market share.
☑ Served as the only team member with knowledge of social media sites and engagement on a consistent basis.

EDUCATION

Bachelor of Business Administration: Marketing
University of Georgia, Athens: 2010

SOFTWARE/TECHNICAL SKILLS

Microsoft Word, Excel & PowerPoint
CRM Tools: Salesforce, Zoho & Pipedrive

VINCENT J. SILVETTI

1234 SW 113th Street | Miami, FL 33176 | jsilvetti@gmail.com | 305-899-1908

SENIOR FINANCIAL ANALYST

PROCESS IMPROVEMENTS – DATA ANALYSIS – FINANCIAL MODELING – VALUATIONS

Accomplished financial analyst with a proven track record in delivering excellence in the analysis of financial, business, and market data to create insightful and highly accurate forecasting. Excels at establishing and sustaining relationships and partnerships with colleagues, clients, managers and other important stakeholders at all levels. Skilled in the development and enhancement of financial modeling and analytical processes along with authoring and presenting reports to senior management, key partners and regulatory organizations.

CORE COMPETENCIES

✓ Goal Achievement	✓ Planning & Forecasting	✓ Key Performance Indicators
✓ Stakeholder Engagement	✓ Variance Analysis	✓ Benchmarking & Assessment
✓ Risk Analysis	✓ Project Management	✓ Documentation & Reporting
✓ Presentation Skills	✓ Strategic Alignment	✓ Financial Best Practices

PROFESSIONAL EXPERIENCE

NORTHEAST BANK WEBSTER, NY   **2016 – PRESENT**
FINANCIAL PLANNING & ANALYSIS (FP&A) SENIOR ANALYST
Consolidate financial results and metrics for the bank and its legal entities; totals $8.5B in assets and $311M in expenses. Develop monthly financial packages, as well as presentations for Senior Managers and Regulators that include variance explanations. Analyze bank sheet activity to equitably split assets and allocate interest expense among existing lines of business (LOB) based on monthly use.

- Led a project that reduced expenses significantly; renegotiated and terminated vendor contracts, which saved the bank millions of dollars.
- Implemented an operating plan and forecast process to ensure that strategic insatiate are aligned with profit targets.
- Spearheaded the development of new processes for reporting, monthly closing and vendor/FTE analysis to reduce expenses.
- Restructured financial hierarchy of the bank and its cost center to align with LOB direction.

BANK OF AMERICA, CHARLOTTE, NC   **2006 – 2016**
VICE PRESIDENT – SENIOR FINANCIAL ANALYST | 2010 – 2016
Liaised with LOB partners to develop a challenging and well-aligned financial plan that supported the company's three-year strategic plan and business goals. Analyzed and produced forecasts and plans for Diversified Serving and Reverse Mortgage; contributed #143M of yearly expenses and over 600 Associates.

- Provided comprehensive analysis to facilitate the understanding of operational KPIs that drove results and lowered risks.
- Identified potential expense reductions to decrease unfavorable variances; allowed for efficient business planning and profitability.
- Constantly lowered cost-to-serve metric results through the effective use of capacity planning.

ASSISTANT VICE PRESIDENT – SENIOR FINANCIAL ANALYST | 2008 – 2010
Prepared and presented financial review packages to LOB executives and team. Compiled and examined the servicing portfolio for Home Equity and other secured/unsecured product loans. Aided in the merger and acquisition of Companywide via mapping financial hierarchies and General Ledger Accounts.

ASSISTANT VICE PRESIDENT-SENIOR FINANCIAL ANALYST | 2008
Supported Retail, Banking Center and other channels by managing monthly and annual expense budgets. Produced and analyzed monthly and annual forecasts and plans for two LOBs.

- Generated ad-hoc financial reports to determine KPIs that would serve to effectively drive results.

OFFICER, FINANCE MANAGEMENT ASSOCIATE PROGRAM (FMAP) – SENIOR FINANCIAL ANALYST | 2007 – 2008
Consolidated and analyzed daily estimates and profit & loss (P&L) statements that contributed to $1B in annual revenue. Reviewed trade positions and complied driver commentaries to Senior Managers on a daily/weekly/monthly basis.

- Reconciled daily balance sheet variances between trading systems and General Ledger.
- Produced, analyzed and presented monthly expense packages for Prime Brokerage and Structured Products.
- Partook in monthly closing by posting journal entries and compiling trend analyses.

OFFICER, FINANCE MANAGEMENT ASSOCIATE PROGRAM (FMAP) –FINANCIAL ANALYST | 2006 – 2007
Actively supported Executives and Managers in the development of reporting packages and investor decks. Consolidated financial results for six LOBs including Real Estate and Credit Cards; contributed $42B in revenue and $19B in annual expenses.

- Headed financial planning, forecasting and month-end closing for all Global Consumer and Small business Banking (GCSBB) products.
- Created and maintained reporting models using Excel and Essbase (Hyperion).
- Allocated monthly entries for various LOBs and posted General Ledger entries.

EDUCATION & TRAINING

Master of Science, Finance, Florida International University (2014)
Bachelor of Business Administration, International Business and MIS, Florida International University (2006)
Also completed training in Financial Reporting, Essbase, Business Partnering and Sig Sigma Green Belt

TECHNOLOGY SKILLS

Microsoft Office Suite (Excel, PowerPoint, Word, Access), Essbase (Hyperion), InSight, IBM Cognos, Oracle

CARA BLANKENSHIP

5543 Polaris LN, Plymouth, MN 55446
612-887-1276 | carab@gmail.com

SENIOR EXECUTIVE OFFICER
LEADERSHIP, VISION, STRATEGY & TACTICAL EXECUTION

Global Executive Officer, specializing in delivering billion-dollar growth through mergers and acquisitions, downsizing, integrations, divestitures, startups, crisis management, capital raises and balance sheet restructures.

SNAPSHOT OF VALUE OFFERED

- **Start Ups:** Catapulted startup Chicago division of Old National Bankcorp from $0 to $3 billion dollars, strongly positioning company for continued international growth.
- **Initial Public Offering:** Rose $40 million in private equity funding to recapitalize Old National, avoiding bankruptcy and saving thousands of jobs.
- **Legal:** Successfully resolved several compliance and governance issues at Klein Bank, including a $14 million SEC claim, FDIC Cease and Desist Order and $1.5 billion class-action lawsuit.
- **Organization Restructure:** Led aggressive restructuring of Klein Bank's Insurance Ventures that saved $250 million.

AREAS OF EXPERTISE

Growth Leadership
Change Management
Restructuring
Six Sigma Training/Black Belt
Negotiation
Chicago MBA
Due Dligence
B2B & B2C

PROFESSIONAL EXPERIENCE

OLD NATIONAL BANCORP | Minneapolis, MN   2014 to Present
A regional bank with over 150 retail branches operated by Old National Bancorp and based in Evansville, Indiana.
Vice President
Chairman Board of Directors
$23.4 Billion | 30 Branches | 1100 Employees
Aggressively recruited from Klein bank to recapitalize, turn around and transform several branches from non-compliance operations to streamlined, customer focused banks. Steer governance, operations and stakeholder matters, overseeing a team of mid-level executives (P&L and Control Leaders) and nine-member Board of Directors.

Provided vision and led execution of several preventative measures ahead of global crisis. Personally expanded liquidity by $800 million, upgraded capital by $300 million, and restructured over 15,000 mortgages.

Action & Results

Continued on Next Page

CARA BLANKENSHIP

Action & Results (continued)

- ⊃ Transformed the business model from mortgage trading activities to retail banking. Added 500,000 retail banking customers while maintaining the #2 position in the mortgage market.
- ⊃ Pioneered the first ever Private Equity investment in a bank holding company in the US and Canada.
- ⊃ Embarked on aggressive cost cutting measure that saved the bank $250 million through workforce reductions and supplier management. Implemented Six Sigma process redesigns.

Personnel Development

- ⊃ Upgraded and developed the entire workforce by replacing the top 3 layers of management and establishing a $2 million leadership training center.
- ⊃ Taught ONB's first and second executive tiers, a five-month Harvard Business School leadership program.

Awards

- ⊃ Recognized with several international awards for campaign to redevelop and re-launch the corporate brand (Corporate Image Transformation, SABRE Award, American Business Award, and PR News).
- ⊃ Heightened visibility of the company, creating numerous award winning community campaigns focused on the environment, empowering women, and expanding cultural and financial literacy.
- ⊃ Received 2013 Minneapolis Chamber of Commerce Award for Excellence in the Banking Sector.

KLEIN BANK | Chaska, MN   2001 - 2014
Operated 21 bank branches. The largest family-owned state bank in Minnesota with assets over $1.9 billion.

Vice President – Consumer Finance | 2010 - 2014
$3 Billion | 6 Countries | 3,000 Employees
Set vision and executed strategies that met and regularly exceeded profit targets for products including: loans (cash, mortgage, commercial), bankcards, sales finance, private label credit, insurance products and loyalty programs distributed through B2B and B2C.

Grew assets and net income from $0 to over $3 billion USD and more than $25 million in earnings. Originated 4+ million consumers; created 12+ new products; built 1000+ in-store branches and 100+ retail branches; and hired and developed 3000+ people.

Action & Results

- ⊃ Positioned company to capture 83% of retail segment.
- ⊃ Acted as a catalyst for the development of several technologies that created sustainable competitive advantages.

EDUCATION

UNIVERSITY OF PENNSYLVANIA, PHILADELPHIA
Master of Business Administration (Executive MBA Program) | 2009
Bachelor of Science in Economics and Finance | 2003

CERTIFICATION

INTERNATIONAL ASSOCIATION FOR SIX SIGMA CERTIFICATION (IASSC) | **Certified Lean Six Sigma Black Belt**

Tiffany White

1432 Steeplechase Pkwy • Marietta, GA 30064 • 678-860-6995 • tiffany1432white@outlook.com

PRIVATE SCHOOL EDUCATOR
8 Years' Success in Meeting the Social, Emotional and Creative Needs of Young Children

Energetic and dedicated teacher with a strong commitment to instilling students with a life-long love of learning. Skilled in integrating music and art into the classroom, providing a creative environment which is interesting and fun for students. Adept in using a variety of teaching methods including hands-on, verbal and visual. Committed to furthering education; hold Technical Certificate of Credit (TCC) in Early Childhood Care and Education.

CORE COMPETENCIES

Music & Art Integration | Differentiated Curriculum | Classroom Management
Child Development | Flexible Lesson Planning | Student Safety | Regulatory Compliance

PROFESSIONAL EXPERIENCE

THE WALKER ACADEMY | Woodstock, GA   2014 – Present
Kindergarten Teacher | 2012 – Present
Teach a class of 12 students in the core areas of math, science and phonics.

- Actively developed and maintain positive parent relationships by communicating student progress on a day-to-day basis.
- Successfully adopted group breakouts for separate instruction, helping children to develop strong communication abilities and tackle complex problems while learning to share perspectives.
- Effectively employed differentiated instruction and tutoring to bring non-readers up to a kindergarten reading level while also meeting the needs of advanced students functioning at a 2nd grade level.

Pre-School Lead Teacher | 2011 – 2012
Taught 3 and 4 year olds with 12-18 students per class.

Proved highly successful engaging children in a safe, organized and stimulating classroom that encouraged creativity, exploration and decision-making. Created a fun learning environment, fostering social and emotional growth.

- Expanded curriculum in collaboration with three fellow Lead Teachers, playing a pivotal role in developing children's full potential by shaping key academic, social and cognitive skills.
- Selected to work with two hearing impaired students with cochlear implants during transition from Speech School into 4-year old class.
  - Observed by Pathologist, receiving praise for voice fluctuation and eye contact that proved key in children's success within traditional classroom setting.

EDUCATION

GEORGIA STATE UNIVERSITY, Atlanta
Bachelor of Art in Sociology | 2011

CERTIFICATION

Chattahoochee Technical College, Marietta, GA
Technical Certificate of Credit (TCC) in Early Childhood Care and Education | 2011

NATASHA HERRINGTON

1233 Canterbury Drive • Atlanta, GA 30326 • 404.563.8650 • tashaatl@outlook.com

ASSISTANT TO DIRECTOR OF ATLANTA METROPOLITAN COMPLEX
Offering a 7-Year Progressive History with Merrill Lynch ... Consistently Producing Stellar Results

Highly organized, results-driven professional with proven track record of administering projects from conception through successful completion. Extremely client-focused with the innate ability to win trust and sustain long-term relationships with internal and external partners. Valued by executives for remaining calm in high-pressure situations, exercising flexibility and confidence to make sound decisions.

CORE COMPETENCIES

Executive Level Administrative Support | Calendar Management | Scheduling
Client Services | Conference Coordination | Event Management | Traveling Planning
Accounts Payable / Accounts Receivables | HR Administrative Assisting

---

PROFESSIONAL EXPERIENCE

MERRILL LYNCH | Atlanta, GA   Sept 2013 – Present
Director's Assistant | July 2012 – Present
Reliable support and liaison for Brookhaven complex Director and over 220 Financial Advisors and Client Advisors covering all 8 Atlanta offices. Entrusted as the only assistant privy to handle highly confidential information.

Complete expense reports and manage all travel arrangements from flights and car rental to lodging. Plan meetings, luncheons and conference calls, including preparing and disseminating materials/correspondence on behalf of the Director. Assist in on-boarding; training new and existing employees.

Designated as first point-of-contact for new hire administration process
- Overhauled offices' hiring system by implementing new processes that resolved numerous issues and significantly improved organization/efficiency of the hiring process.
- Play key role in on-boarding new recruits from other financial firms; compile and enter paperwork to ensure a smooth transition.
- Elevated level of security and accountability by refining the new-hire finger printing and background check process; expedited transmission of information to verifying agencies.
- Recognized for keeping HR files organized and up to date; accurately enter all hiring, salary changes and terminations in database.
- Prove successful in handling large volume of HR requests including compensation and incentives.

Praised by Director for the smooth functionality of all events, advancing responsibility to include planning and scheduling meetings, including high-level conference calls
- Successfully manage busy schedule, ensuring Director attends all scheduled conference calls with zero conflicts.

Recognized expert in Practice Management Development (PMD) training, aiding in successful transition from office to Bank of America
- Appointed to teach Practice Management Development (PMD) training to employees on tract to become Financial Advisors.

Manager's Assistant | Nov 2011 – July 2012
Provided high-level assistance to three Office Managers, including executing regular seminars and meetings.
- Valued for assisting management in daily operations, which proved instrumental in maintaining optimal workflow and productivity.
- Hand selected to lead special project arranging floor plans for all six offices that included 250 employees and 250 workstations.

Continued on next page ...

188

PROFESSIONAL EXPERIENCE CONTINUED

TRC STAFFING | Atlanta, GA   July 2011 – Sept 2011
Administrative Assistant
Assigned to provide administrative support and manage a multi-line phone system for 50 clients at Lang Lasalle, a commercial real estate company.
- Entrusted to administer billing for all clients, including variable and fixed charges.
- Cultivated communication pipeline for clients by designing and generating a bi-monthly newsletter.
- Coordinated and executed a large volume of client meetings and conferences including: creating materials, gathering RSVPs, handling food/beverage logistics and managing guest registration.

AXION| Atlanta, GA   July 2009 – May 2011
Temporary Executive Assistant
Quickly built reputation for providing superior assistance to company executives; repeatedly requested by numerous companies within construction, shipping and various other industries.
- Provided instrumental assistance in supporting ongoing needs during five-day retreat attended by hundreds of people; contributions included assembling materials and managing attendees.
- Effectively organized multiple responsibilities to manage daily office needs and multi-line telephone systems for numerous businesses.

CHASE, WHITEHEAD & GARDNER, LLP | Atlanta, GA   Sept 2004 – Feb 2009
Conference Service Assistant | Sept 2005 – Feb 2009
Aggressively recruited to permanent status after completing dual internships with the company. Assigned to newly created position managing 30 conference rooms. Served on various committees including: Wellness, First-Aid Certification, Breast Cancer Awareness and Staff Appreciation.
- Played pivotal role in building a web-based program that included a survey and enabled people to request items needed such as materials/supplies, floor plans and directories prior to arriving onsite at the office.
- Collaborated with Project Manager and Attorneys to close a multi-billion deal.
- Earned distinction as point-of-contact for all departmental events including: HR, Professional Development and Marketing.
- Valued for committee involvement, contributions included: gathering employees for daily walks, and handling catering, decorating and planning for Staff appreciation week.
- Developed and implemented new traditions at the firm, earning high acclaim from managers and employees.

EDUCATION

UNIVERSITY OF NORTH CAROLINA | Charlotte
Bachelor of Science in Business Administration | 2003
Associate of Science in Executive Administrative Assisting | 2002

TECHNICAL SKILLS

Microsoft Word, Excel and PowerPoint; CRM
Inter Office Software: WMW+| RazorGator | Concur (expense reporting system) | My HR

SEAN ESQUIRE

4332 Midlothian Road
Bloomfield Hills, MI 48302

Phone: (248) 536-1987
seanesquire@comcast.net

REGIONAL SALES MANAGER
Specializing in multimillion-dollar profit growth for the health care industry

MEDICAL DEVICE SALES / CAPITAL EQUIPMENT SALES

Top performing B2B sales professional with a 14+ career track record of growing regions and territories for Animas, a Johnson & Johnson company, as well as other entities in the medical devices space. Creative and exemplary leader with a passion for sales leadership, keen business acumen, strong planning and organizational skills and high level of achievement. Proven record of developing sales teams for maximum performance while meeting bottom-line results.

MAJOR COMPETENCIES

- Strategic Planning & Execution	- Business Development	- Sales Forecasting
- Territory Analysis	- Process Improvement	- Consultative Selling
- Program Management	- Sales Team Coaching	- Customer Relationship Building
- Negotiations	- Account Management	- Resource Allocation

PRODUCT EXPERTISE

Parentral/Ambulatory Infusion Devices ▶ Insulin Pumps/Consumer Based Products
Medical Solutions Filtration Devices ▶ OEM

PROFESSIONAL EXPERIENCE

ANIMAS CORPORATION, WEST CHESTER, PA   **2008-PRESENT**
A Johnson & Johnson company specializing in insulin pumps for diabetes patients. Company offers a first generation automated system for managing Type I diabetes, infusion sets, wireless and manual systems.

Great Lakes Regional Manager (2010-present)

Develop and implement strategic sales plans to attain corporate goals and achieve/surpass sales quota. Oversee sales forecasting and attainment of performance goals. Recruit, hire, train, develop, coach and mentor a total of 10 reports.

- Built territory into a top territory and rapidly advanced to regional manager.
- Mastered *Integrity Selling* and other training courses such as *Leader Manager* since Johnson & Johnson acquisition.

Record for Plan Rank for the Last Several Years

2012	2014	2016	2017	2018
101% to plan	103% to plan	117.4% to plan	92.6% to plan	96% to plan
Rank 3 out of 6	Rank 2 out of 8	Rank 1 out of 10	Rank 3 out of 10	Rank 5 out of 10

Midwest Regional Sales Manager (2006-2010)

Actively directed sales activities of 10 representatives in the Midwestern and New England regions.

- Led region to revenue growth of $8 million in insulin pumps in less than two years.
- Expanded territories to seven states: Illinois, Indiana, Iowa, Michigan, Minnesota, Ohio and W. Virginia.
- Accelerated new business development through initiation of corporate account partnerships.

ADDITIONAL ACCOMPLISHMENTS AND AWARDS

- Recognized as a sales training leader. Led a series of Wilson Learning "Counselor Salesperson", "Versatile Salesperson" and strategic selling programs for more than 30 field sales representatives.
- Built Midwest Region into the #1 revenue producing territory in the national sales organization – delivered in excess of 30% of total corporate revenues.
- Personally closed four exclusive national sales contracts with major medical providers that generated $5.2 million in company revenues.
- President's Club recipient five years consecutively.
- Won "Best Trainer of the Year" award six years in a row.
- Selected as Key Territory Manager of the Mid-West region for Animas after only 1 month of training. The first ever sales associate to be promoted this soon/
- Recently tapped to take over Director's role upon his retirement.

EDUCATION

Bachelor of Arts: Communications, Michigan State University

Sonia Lockett

559 Teresita Blvd. | San Francisco, CA 94127
(415) 515-2671| soniarlockett1@gmail.com

Marketing & Public Relations

Highly organized self-starter with extensive experience in the hospitality, music, film and entertainment industries. Able to think outside the box and develop compelling campaigns that reach targeted markets.

Career Highlights & Key Areas of Value to Your Organization

- Demonstrated success in managing high-profile events, including those for MTV Networks.
- Provided top-notch performance and efficiency with administrative support for The Hit Factory.
- Built up clientele and forged numerous profitable relationships throughout career.
- Media savvy and thoroughly knowledgeable of social media networks and marketing technology.
- Passionate about current lifestyle and cultural trends relevant to today's multi-cultural, urban and mainstream millennial consumer and industry trendsetters.
- Strong knowledge of the PR field including experience in media relations, press campaign development and execution of creative and strategic communication plans.
- Effective time management and multitasking skills; able to work under pressure in time sensitive environme

Core Competencies

- Marketing & Promotions
- Strategic Planning & Execution
- SEO, SEM and PPC Campaigns
- Branding & Strategizing
- Media Relations

- Working with A-List Clients & Executives
- Event Planning / Event Management
- Budgeting, Forecasting & Analysis
- Product management and Development
- Strong Writing Skills/Press Releases

Software Skills: Microsoft Word, PowerPoint, Excel and Outlook; Google Analytics; Adobe Photoshop

Professional Experience and Accomplishments

Marketing

- Served as marketing Representative for the Xen Lounge in Studio City, CA. Successfully planned all events,, developed press releases and distributed to various media outlets and advertising agencies.
- Effectively managed client database and assisted the CEO with administrative tasks, scheduling meetings, follow-up phone calls to new leads as well as existing clients.
- Devised a $60K budgeting plan for an innovative marketing strategy to promote this start-up venue.
- Hosted a major event with nearly 700 attendees. Consisted of up and coming actors/actresses and celebrities.

Public Relations

- On boarded as a key member of the Silicon Valley Film Festival and assisted in planning the entire event for eight years. Participated in board meetings at the State Capitol. Accountable for budgeting and promotions.
- Managed a wide range of PR activities, including contacting advertising outlets, setting up on-site and off-site promotional stands near local campuses.
- Launched an aggressive promotional campaign that brought awareness and garnered the participation of thousands of students to the festival.

Continued on Next Page…

Public Relations Continued-

MTV Networks Logo Press:
- Engaged in extensive PR activities to market MTV's awards show. Developed press kits, social media strategies and served as a liaison between guests, producers and sponsors.
- Played an integral role in leading a press conference for the "Sordid Lives" show, in addition to board meetings to discuss marketing development and promotional plans.
- Instrumental in scheduling appointments with A-list clients to continue generating more press for MTV.

Administrative Support
- Served as the Receptionist and first point of contact for The Hit Factory Criteria's clients and engineers.
- Effectively managed in-bound phone calls, all mail, including emails and correspondence. Scheduled artists for various studio rooms, delegated food runs and ensured timely room service for clients.
- Managed client database and ensured all history remained current.

Employment History

Xen Lounge | Studio City, CA   2013 – 2018
Marketing Representative

Palace Hotel | San Francisco, CA   2010 – 2013
Marketing Assistant

The Hit Factory- Criteria Recording Studios | Los Angeles, CA   2009 – 2010
Administrative Assistant

Education

Bachelor of Arts: Public Relations | 2010 | Sonoma State University | Rohnert Park, CA

Professional Membership Organizations

Toastmasters- Member of the Bay City location in San Francisco.

ROSHONDA WILLIAMS

3222 Treeline Drive | Decatur, Georgia 30058 | Cell: 678-535-4328 | rhashondawilliams@comcast.net

ACCOUNTING MANAGER

Proven Success in Financial Process Improvement for Child Nutrition Programs

Meticulous accounting professional with a verifiable record of accomplishments over a progressive career with Decatur Public Schools and the Georgia Department of Education. Experienced in all aspects of accounting, budgeting, forecasting, financial analysis and reporting for various multimillion-dollar governmental agencies. An innovative problem solver with the ability to design and execute robust internal accounting controls with accurate reporting and regulatory compliance.

Areas of Expertise

✓ GAAP & GASB Compliance	✓ Program Consulting	✓ Continuous Process Improvement
✓ Financial Management	✓ Grants Accounting	✓ Federal/State/Local Regulations
✓ Policy & Procedure Development	✓ Financial Statements	✓ Supply Chain Management
✓ Cost Accounting	✓ Purchasing	✓ Staff Training & Supervision
✓ Account Reconciliation	✓ Contracts Administration	✓ External Vendor Relationships

HIGHLIGHTS OF CAREER ACCOMPLISHMENTS

Decatur Public Schools
- Delivered $97,000 in cost savings and improved supply chain management by developing and implementing the district's delivery tracker for USDA commodities inventory.
- Participated in the State of Georgia pilot for the new Fresh Fruit and Vegetable program online claim and reporting system. Improved operational efficiency and increased program revenues by $1 million.
- Developed and implemented a $35 million budget for several nutrition programs through adequate forecasting.
- Piloted a number of training programs for management team and food service contractors.

Awards
- 2016 Georgia and USDA Southeast Regional Best Practice Awards; fiscal management innovations for improving plate costs.

PROFESSIONAL EXPERIENCE

DECATUR PUBLIC SCHOOLS 2008 – PRESENT

Accounting Manager 2009 – Present | $22 Million Contract | Compliance Division | 4 Direct reports
Steer overall financial management for the school district's Nutrition department consisting of 51,000 students and 84 feeding sites. Manage $1.4 million in USDA food inventory, along with order processing and distribution of products. Develop and deliver training on department procedures, accounting and POS software processes, budget, inventory and financial management. Charged with additional daily tasks for the following areas:

Accounting / Internal Control / Regulatory Compliance
- Provide leadership and coaching to two accountants, two accounting clerks and guide team in state, federal and local government regulatory compliance, accurate recording of revenues, expenditures, assets, liabilities and inventories for the following programs:
  - National School Lunch, School Breakfast Program, the After-School Snack Program, Supper Program, Fresh Fruit and Vegetable Grants and others through the USDA.
- Oversee monthly/year-end general ledger reconciliation and close processes. Establish internal controls for reliable meal accountability systems that produce accurate claims for reimbursement and annual revenues.
- Develop accounting and reporting system requirements that impact all nutrition programs.
- Assist with annual external audit, state and federal administrative reviews. Prepare assigned schedules for the annual and interim audit.

Continued on Next Page...

Budget & Cash Management
- Develop and control several nutrition program budgets totaling $35 million.
- Monitor cash transactions, ensure bank balances are reconciled to the general ledger cash balance and investigate any unusual items. Oversee the preparation of cash flow reports, identify and evaluate variances.

Contract Administration and Procurement
- Monitor and evaluate multiple contract vendors to ensure compliance with fiscal laws and procedures. Execute change recommendations for operational efficiency. Includes the following contracts: $22 million food service management, $350,000 equipment repair and $200,000 cleaning contracts.

Financial Analysis and Reporting
- Conduct complex financial analysis; review data trends, forecasting, compile reports to identify system deficiencies.
- Prepare financial management reports to assist decision makers in determining profitability, program efficiency, and for discovering areas for improvement. Communicate findings with Nutrition Executive Director and C-level management team.

Key Accomplishments

- Assumed role as Crisis Manager; developed and designed a highly efficient system for submitting delinquent claims for reimbursements for the previous fiscal year and aided in submitting future claims for reimbursement to Georgia Department of Education.
  Results: Nutrition department recovered $12 million in lost revenue, increased department's overall profitability, and enhanced operational efficiency.
- Served as subject matter expert for meal counting, claim reporting and methods to improve state reporting.
  Results: Department met reporting deadline and improved profitability. Provided vendor with a new module to sell to future customers.
- Defined business processes, policies and regulatory requirements during development of a new nutrition accounting module for the district; LAWSON ERP system.
- Implemented a new data processing cost accounting system for school nutrition that significantly improved accuracy and timeliness for submitting financial reports to State Department.
- Enhanced operational efficiency as project manager on the chart of accounts redesign team.
- Earned reimbursement for claims resulting in more than $24 million.

EDUCATION

MERCER UNIVERSITY, Atlanta, GA
Master of Business Administration

GEORGIA STATE UNIVERSITY, Atlanta, GA
Bachelor of Business: Accounting and Marketing

COMPUTER/SOFTWARE SKILLS

Microsoft Word, Excel, PowerPoint; Lawson Financial, Heartland Nutrition; Web-based Supply Chain Management

CERTIFICATION

ServSafe Certification: 2015 – 2020

PROFESSIONAL ORGANIZATIONS

School Nutrition Association (SNA)

CHADWICK MOSELY

1666 Peachtree Street | Atlanta, Georgia 30308 | Cell: 770-435-4333| chadmosely@gmail.com

Social Security Number: [xxx-xx-xxxx] ▪ Citizenship: U.S.
Veterans Preference: 10 Points

Transportation Assistant
Vacancy Announcement Number: [xxxx]

MANAGEMENT PROFESSIONAL

Dependable, highly skilled leader and U.S. Army Veteran with 10 years of progressive experience in transportation management and logistics, as well as training and developing peers for superior performance. Built an honorable professional history focused on core values with integrity first, while consistently striving for excellence. Offering strong organizational skills and attention to detail for high level of operational efficiency.

CORE COMPETENCIES

Management Operations | Logistical Planning & Management | Procurement | Vendor Sourcing
Strategic Planning & Implementation | Contract Management | Negotiations | Staff Management
Veterans Agency Support | Customer Service | Effective Communications | Problem Solving

EXPERIENCE HIGHLIGHTS

Transportation

➤ Assisted thousands of veterans as the Transportation Assistant for Department of Veteran Affairs. Steered daily operations of the Beneficiary Travel Program.
➤ Implemented a new processing method that reduced wait time from 60 days down to 14.
➤ Experienced in fleet management transportation/dispatching for a $9 billion retail/petroleum entity.
➤ Served as Transportation Management Coordinator for the U.S. Army and successfully prepared travel itineraries, personal property shipping documents and passenger movement forms in a timely manner.

Contracts/Procurement

➤ Served as a Contract Specialist for World Technical Services managing firm fixed-price contracts. Developed skills in bid solicitation, negotiating and procurement.
➤ Completed a multitude of professional training courses in procurement, purchasing and vendor management.
➤ Played an integral role as a member of the Acquisition Management Review Team. Successfully delivered the most current data reports to Senior Management.

EMPLOYMENT HISTORY

RACETRAC PETROLEUM

Transportation Dispatcher   01/2016 – 04/2019
3225 Cumberland Blvd.   Salary: $50,000/Yr.
Suite 100   Hours per week: 40+
Atlanta, GA 30339
Supervisor: Billy Sykes (470) 455-5666
Monitored 100+ franchise stores and inventory levels throughout the Southeast, in addition to managing and dispatching drivers to refuel various locations. Coordinated with other trucking companies for on time delivery. Maximized time to ensure as many routes were completed as possible. Determined best times for dispatching based on stores' activity, needs and local traffic. Ensured stores remained at optimum levels at all times. Immediately handled any potential obstacle to prevent downtime.

CHADWICK MOSELY

chadmosely@gmail.com

DEPARTMENT OF VETERAN AFFAIRS

Transportation Assistant
7400 Merton Minter
San Antonio, TX 78229
Supervisor: Frank Thomas (210) 617-5300

02/2015 – 01/2016
Salary: $45,944/Yr.
Hours per week: 40

Administered the Beneficiary Travel Program that provides transportation services to beneficiaries and their attendants traveling to and from VA facilities and other locations for examinations, treatment or care. Screened veterans for eligibility and assisted with completing the travel benefits application.

Provided excellent customer service whether communicating in-office, by phone, fax or email. Interacted with patients, family members, private sector medical facilities and VA staff. Instrumental in arranging all modes of transportation in a timely manner. Included air ambulance, commercial air, taxi, bus or independent transportation. Managed any special arrangements related to patients' medical condition per physician notes. Demonstrated strong attention to detail when reviewing travel request cost analysis and remained in compliance with all regulations.

WORLD TECHNICAL SERVICES

Contract Specialist
4903 NW Industrial Blvd.
San Antonio, TX 78238
Supervisor: Cary Garza (210) 364-7184

03/2014 – 01/2015
Salary: $32,000/Yr.
Hours per week: 40

Served as a key member managing the Center for Healthcare Services contract, one of the largest contracts obtained by this non-profit organization for the disabled. Directed a wide range of tasks including, the bidding process, procurement of goods and services, negotiated and administered contracts. Solicited sources of supply and analyzed the following: prices, discount rates, delivery dates, transportation charges, previous performance and recommended the best offer. Instrumental in analyzing business practices and market conditions to evaluate bid responsiveness, contractor responsibility and contractor performance.

Spearheaded a 12 month development project for the Center for Healthcare Services valued at $3 to $5 million. Consisted of recruiting and placing janitorial personnel at 20 facilities along with supplies for each location. Effectively managed all employees and millions of dollars in inventory. Completed project on time and under budget.

TEXAS HEALTH AND HUMAN SERVICES COMMISSION (HHSC)

Case Manager
IH 35 N
San Antonio, TX 78227
Supervisor: Enrique Olivarez (210) 619-8006

05/2013 – 01/2014
Salary: $30,000/Yr.
Hours per week: 40

Managed an average of 50 cases consisting of applicants and recipients of TANA, Medicaid and other social service programs. Conducted financial consultations, benefits eligibility and the appeals process. Explained income standards thoroughly to clients, verified documentation and submitted in a timely manner. Consulted clients and served as their first point of contact from initial application through entire length of services. Remained in constant communication with clients; provided regular ongoing status of their case. Reconciled overpayments and adjustments to ensure clients received accurate amount of benefits. Conducted annual reviews of benefit packages to keep case files current. Effectively led the appeal process whenever a clients' service lapsed, additional information was requested or application denied. Gathered all necessary information and submitted for fair hearing process.

CHADWICK MOSELY

chadmosely@gmail.com

UNITED HEALTHCARE

Health Advisor

05/2012 – 04/2013

6200 Northwest Parkway

Salary: $28,000/Yr.

San Antonio, TX 78249

Hours per week: 40

Supervisor: Carlos Medrano (210) 478-4800

Managed a high volume of calls/inquiries regarding healthcare benefits for a large call center environment. Worked on a team of 10-15 members and handled over 100 calls daily. Demonstrated effective listing, consultative and problem solving skills while handling customers' needs. Researched procedures, diagnostic and ICD-9 codes to determine coverage. Documented all calls thoroughly. Mastered the use of all internal UHC systems within a short time span and resolved the most complex healthcare related questions for both customers and providers.

U.S. ARMY

Transportation Management Coordinator

04/2001 – 01/2011

491st ACD

Salary: $36,000/Yr.

Fort Eustis, VA 23604

Hours per week: 40

Supervisor: Milton Chamblee (757) 726-3466

Provided ongoing training and instruction to soldiers on assisting military members with travel itineraries, personal property shipping documents and passenger movement forms. Processed transport capability requests to meet mission movements during training which provided well-rounded knowledge to team members. Instrumental in records management which included labeling cargo and freight shipments, documenting and managing freight inventory, cargo and various material shipments. Consistently updated information on software programs such as TC-AIMS, TC-AIMS II and WPS. Served as a Human Resource Specialist and managed a wide range of administrative tasks including coordinating requests for evaluations, ceremonies and promotions. Prepared and delivered technical reports, correspondence, presentations and meeting minutes. Oversaw personnel management tasks including the processing of personnel security clearance, record updates and orders for change of duty station; temporary and permanent. Oversaw additional requests such as: identification cards, tags, leaves, line of duty determination, MILPER data and information management.

EDUCATION

TEXAS A&M UNIVERSITY, San Antonio, TX
Bachelor of Business Administration: Management: 2016

PROFESSIONAL TRAINING & DEVELOPMENT

Certifying Officials of Commercial Invoices	06/2018
Procurement Overview Course	07/2018
Procurement Process Course	07/2017
Procurement Pre-Solicitation/Solicitation Course	07/2017
Award Preparations/Award/Post-Award/Closeout Course	07/2017
Proposal Evaluations Course	07/2016
Purchasing and Vendor Management	07/2014
Government Contracting Essentials Course	07/2011
Professional Leadership Course	04/2009

ANGEL M. THOMPSON
11018 John J. Delaney Drive • Charlotte, NC 28262
704-455-1455 • angelthompson221@gmail.com

Social Security Number: xxx-xx-xxxx • Citizenship: U.S.
Veterans Preference: 5 Points
Secret Security Clearance

Support Services Specialist
Job Announcement Number: NCAF 12-26

➤ Diligent, self-motivated professional with over 18 years of loyal service to the Air National Guard in North Carolina and New York, currently serving as a Knowledge Operations Manager, MSgt.

➤ Dedicated to providing outstanding technical and administrative support within diverse environments.

➤ Distinguished track record in performing complex office duties, utilizing word processing skills to reformat lengthy correspondence/reports, create and maintain spreadsheets and databases.

➤ Advanced ability to multi-task, seeking different approaches and methods to meet specific assignment requirements.

➤ Experienced in food service and medical support.

CORE COMPETENCIES

Administrative Support Services | Mail Operating Systems | File Maintenance
Drafting Correspondence, Forms & Reports | Records Management | Scheduling
Confidentiality of Files & Records | Timekeeping | Strong Typing Skills | Training
Spreadsheet & Database Management | Supervisory Skills | Travel Planning

PROFESSIONAL EXPERIENCE

AIR NATIONAL GUARD

Knowledge Operations Manager; MSgt

Traditional Guardsmen
263rd Combat Communications Squadron (CBCS)
39563 Warrior Way
New London, NC
Supervisor: Ms. Sandra Baker 704-498-2008, May Contact: Yes

07/2011 – Present
Annual Salary: $58,890.00
Hours: 1 weekend/month &
15 days training/year

Provide general administrative support and technical advice on section functions, serving as the first point of contact for 225 base personnel and supervising officials on records management, CitiBank travel card and Freedom of Information Act. Guide and process new enlistments, re-enlistments and separation actions. Oversee training and supervision of two subordinates.

Maintain lodging database, orderly room and conference room scheduling. Prepare and type correspondence, forms, letters, message and documents (classified and unclassified). Review and edit all correspondence to ensure proper format, spelling, punctuation and grammar.

Continued on next page

Training
- Conducted training on government travel card and tracked associated activity to ensure compliance with yearly training requirement for 50-100 unit personel.
- Selected to deliver new hire orientation training on recording leave, time keeping and FOIA.
- Designated as subject matter expert and key trainer on file records management; conducted annual Staff Assisted visit to ensure records were current.
  - Wrote report findings detailing whether unit met training requirements or required additional training.
- Recognized for improving subordinate performance and efficiency by delivering training on job duties, program requirements and compliance.

Service Support
- Identified potential fraudulent activities on CitiBank travel card and notified Sergeant/Commandor; followed up with superiors on status of all inquiries.
- Entrusted by Commander to oversee Management Internal Control Tracking program database in preparation for Unit Compliance Inspection.
- Tracked publications on spreadsheet; sent out emails to leadership regarding publication/form due for review of current publication. Created revised forms, ensuring correct format and routed to each section organization wide.

Special Programs
- Recognized as subject matter expert on travel systems, travel vouchers and training (group one on one); send regular emails on new regulations.
- Implemented procedures that significantly improved lodging program; sent out mass emails regarding lodging cut off dates, new lodging procedures, rates and participating locations to meet changing program requirements.
- Communicated with superiors regarding delinquent payments; made recommendations to revoke individuals lodging priveleges revoked.
- Developed Excel spreadsheet for travel card, tracking individual training and dates. Implemented prior authorization requirement to ensure guidelines/requirements were met prior to ordering government travel card.
- Collaborate with medical squadron to ensure all medical requirements are maintained and up to date; generate detailed report to disseminate information to individual and supervisor regarding appointment time and location.

Freedom of Privacy Act
- Appointed to serve as unit monitor for Freedom of Information Act (FOIA); attended intensive training, in turn delivered associated training for all unit personnel on document handling and privacy.
- Developed PowerPoint enabling daily tracking of required training to ensure compliance during inspections.
- Disseminate regular updates on FOIA changes via email and implemented postings in each office providing personal point of contact information.

Key Accomplishments
- Championed successful effort that updated backlogged records spanning over a decade; completed initiative within two months of appointment.

Continued on next page

- Played integral role in successful overseas deployment of 50 personnel in 2011; processed orders, travel vouchers, lodging, time cards and pay documents.
  - Proved instrumental in preventing payment delays despite changes in start dates; improved process by setting up pay prior to actual deployment.
- Championed effort to ensure zero balance on outstanding travel vouchers prior to new fiscal year; disseminated information to section supervisors and executed follow up.
- Recognized by commanding officer with award for assisting 145th Family Readiness Unit with administrative duties and tracking all phone calls accordingly.

Airman & Family Readiness Assistant; MSgt

Temporary AGR Tour   11/2011 – 06/2012
North Carolina Air National Guard   Ending Annual Salary: $55,000
4930 Minuteman Way   Hours Per Week: 40
Charlotte, NC 28208
Supervisor: Mr. Henderson 704-398-4949, May Contact: Yes

Served as assistant to the 145th Airlift Wing, Airman & Family Readiness Coordinator. Provided administrative support with Readiness Programs including maintaining a database of 310 service members and 115 deployed personnel. Managed event and base supply purchases and associated budgets. Assembled program materials and disseminated internal and external communications.

- Proved successful in coordinating nine events over seven months with 599 service members and family members in attendance.
- Served as readiness point of contact, providing a variety of services and programs to assist active duty military, their family members, retirees and DoD civilians in achieving success and adapting to the military way of life.

Management and Program Assistant; GS-7

Air Guard Technician   10/2008 – 05/2011
New York Air National Guard   Ending Annual Salary: $51,000
9910 Blewett Ave   Hours Per Week: 40
Niagara Falls, NY 14304
Supervisor: James Kwiatkowski 716-353-3276, May Contact: Contact me first

Administered and determined effectiveness of support programs including readiness, lodging, survivor assistance and office automation; initiated and recommended action for improving and implementing program policies and procedures. Served as the Services Safety representative; attended meetings and ensured associated standards were met within services. Resolved contract discrepancies, partnering with accounting program manager to integrate and reconcile orders.

- Played instrumental role in procurement of subsistence for UTA weekend, which included meeting with vendor, placing order, and reviewing menu and food order.
- Improved food service inventory management through procuring new program that tracked inventory in storeroom.
- Recognized for executing online training program that effectively trained Honor Guard in FLO and SAP without requiring group forum.
- Exercised sound judgment and employed innovative approaches that creatively resolved problems in absence of specific guidance.

Continued on next page

Administrative Assistant; GS-7   10/2000 – 8/2008
New York Air National Guard   Ending Annual Salary: $50,000
9910 Blewett Ave   Hours Per Week: 40
Niagara Falls, NY 14304
Supervisor: James Kwiatkowski 716-353-3276, May Contact: Yes

Provided technical and administrative support to 300 personnel, two commanders and one executive officer, serving as first line of communication. Controlled scheduling, conference meetings, visitor support, travel and accommodations. Drafted reports for Air Commander's approval and submission.

- Played integral role in managing the Internal Management Control Program (IMCP); established suspense system, drafted annual wing plan and provided accurate information on program changes and status of IMCP submission by managers.
- Developed analysis tools using data report findings; identified trends and advised leaders on systematic strengths and weaknesses. Provided associated coaching to managers on IMCP.
- Maintained optimal operational function by making sound recommendations to resolve ongoing problems; developed inspection schedules and reviewed reports to identify problems areas.

EDUCATION

CASE COMMUNITY COLLEGE, ELON COLLEGE, NC
Associate in Arts ~ Liberal Arts/Social Science, 01/2011

COMMUNITY COLLEGE OF THE AIR FORCE, Maxwell-Gunter AFB, AL
Associate in Applied Science ~ Information Management Specialty, 06/2008

TRAINING

- Mortuary Affairs Management, 07/2016
- Food Management, 07/2015
- Emergency Management for FEMA National Response Framework, 07/2013
- FEMA National Incident Management Systems, 07/2012
- Initial Actual Incident, 07/2010
- Introduction to Incident Command Systems, 07/2010
- Prime Ribs Management, 03/2010
- Fatality Search & Recovery Team, 06/2010
- North Carolina National Guard Common Drug Task Force Training, 08/2009

AWARDS

Global War on Terrorism Service Medal (Campaign Badge)
Formal Recognition from Commander for Assisting the 145th Family Readiness Unit

JENNIFER KLINE

klinejen@gmail.com

1566 battlefield Dr. NW | Acworth, GA 30102 | C: 678-415-3456 | H: 678-778-0099

CORE COMPETENCIES

Crisis Intervention | Managing Stressful Conditions | Behavioral & Developmental Health
Client Monitoring & Supervision | Team Leadership & Motivation | Assistant & Independent Living
Person Centered Practices | Counseling & Training | Patient/Family Education | Reporting & Documentation

PROFESSIONAL EXPERIENCE

CHEROKEE TRAINING CENTER | Canton, GA

2013 – Present

Direct Support Professional

- ► Assist six to eight developmentally disabled clients per day with daily lifestyle and self-care. Supervise participants during all program activities and ensure supported individuals are actively engaged in preferred activities.
- ► Report unusual or disruptive behavior. Support individuals by utilizing Person Centered Practices and People First language.
- ► Instrumental in providing ongoing appropriate assistance in all activities of supported clients and in helping them to achieve their goals. Includes self-sufficiency, cleanliness, safety and comfort.
- ► Managed various clients' disruptive behavior by redirecting their conduct which has prevented injury to themselves and others.
- ► Document activities thoroughly and accurately. Complete incident and accident reports as necessary within established timeframes.
- ► Successful in preparing for audits and consistently passing with 98% or better.
- ► Earned excellent ratings on performance reviews and duly noted for adhering to HIPPA laws and compliance.

THE NORTH COBB TREATMENT CENTER | Acworth, GA

2007 – 2013

Direct Support Professional

- ► Provided treatment and care for an average of 20 adolescents with behavioral issues. Monitored and supervised clients and guided them in all aspects of daily living.
- ► Effectively managed and monitored daily progress of each client and completed all written documentation.
- ► Prevented all clients from harm by following all safety and disaster plans.
- ► Received Certificate of Appreciation for a strong work ethic and for going above and beyond.

THE CENTER FOR DEVELOPMENT DISABILITIES | Atlanta, GA

2001 – 2007

Employment Training Specialist-Supported Employment: 2002 – 2007

- ► Played an integral role in helping developmentally disabled clients secure employment and maximize their capabilities by training, screening and evaluating for community-based positions.
- ► Worked directly with employers in selecting candidates and placing them on assignments.
- ► Regularly visited clients on the job to ensure successful continuance of employment.
- ► Developed periodic written reports on clients' progress and presented during monthly and annual meetings.
- ► Received Employee of the Month for outstanding job performance in 2001.
- ► Honored with several letters of recommendation.
- ► Earned Certificate of Recognition in 2000 and 2001 for loyalty of service.

Developmental Specialist/Assistant/Activities Coach and Training Coordinator: 2000 – 2001

- ► Supervised and trained developmentally delayed adults on basic work and habilitative activities.
- ► Led community outings to increase clients' independence and documented monthly progress.

EDUCATION

Bachelor of Science: Sociology: 2017 | GEORGIA STATE UNIVERSITY | Atlanta
Associate of Science: Business Administration | Georgia Perimeter College | Dunwoody

CERTIFICATION

Certificate: Direct Service Care for People with Developmental Disabilities: 2004

JASON "JAY" MAYS

(770-885-5783 | jaymaysconstruction@gmail.com
4555 August Lane | Denver, CO 80210

SENIOR CONSTRUCTION MANAGER

Construction Leadership: 20+ years of global experience in driving all aspects of the construction lifecycle, from sourcing new clients and markets, contract negotiation, project planning, design and build for commercial, industrial, and government clients. Skilled in creating a competitive advantage by identifying business differentiators in new market and negotiating/closing sales.

Business Leader: Demonstrated talent in establishing and growing organizations, driving revenue growth of $300M+. Innovative leader with natural ability to analyze business needs and create high-impact solutions. Talented in building and managing staff, driving team empowerment and creating harmony across business units.

Project Management: Delivered projects utilizing Design/Build, General Construction, Program Management, and At Risk methodologies. Experienced in hands-on project management and deep-dives into project performance and recovery analysis.

Sustainability / Green Expert: Deep knowledge of sustainable solutions.

Value to your Organization
Design Build/Projects
Client Relationship Management
General Contractor Projects
Risk Mitigation
P&L Management
Sourcing Strategies & Solutions
Budget Management
Strategic Management/Direction
Sales / Negotiation Skills
Presentations

Design and build of the following projects:

Industrial: East Coast Olive Oil, process removal and relocation ($18M), Medical Sterilization Facility ($20M), Ventura Foods ($3M), Blue Diamond Processing Plant ($14M), RAB food process and bakery relocation ($16), MTD Semi-Automated Distribution Center ($20M), Associated Grocers Dry and Cold Storage ($15M), Sarah Lee ($5M)

Education: Kennesaw State Academic Building and Performing Arts ($30M), DeKalb Technical College ($24M), Georgia Southern ($40M)

Government: Parking Decks ($25M), Cherokee County Admin and Conference Center ($24M), Paulding County Courthouse and Administration ($62M) Kankakee Detention Center ($15M), Pickens County Jail ($8M)

Selected Projects

Fresh & Easy:	Provided construction leadership for design and build of $130M Tesco food processing, cold storage and distribution facility.
Health Key:	Managed the Renal Products Spinning and Winding Facility for Kidney Dialysis, a $50M project.
Guam K-12:	Provided Program Management for the construction of four schools in South Pacific, a $70M project.
Atlanta K-12:	Selected for renovation and addition of middle school and high school, a $60M project; Renovated and built addition for two Fulton County schools, a $30M project.
Detention Center:	Directed build for the Bibb County Detention Center, a $40M project.

Professional Experience

GEORGIA STATE UNIVERSITY (Atlanta, GA) .... Nov. 2015 – Present
RESEARCH & DEVELOPMENT CENTER FOR GREEN BUILDING
A new research center creating practical and sustainable solutions for world-wide green building, supply chain, and technology transformation.

CAO/FOUNDER
Founded research center to connect students and businesses in learning opportunities in green building environment. Assist the Cobb County Schools in certification of first Leadership in Energy and Environmental Design (LEED).

Key Achievements:
- **Atlanta Better Buildings Challenge**. Charged with managing Technical/Benchmarking, Buyer's Guide and Procurement Facilitation committees to drive a 20% savings in water and energy consumption by 2020. Project includes working with Atlanta Mayor's Office, Central Atlanta Progress Department of Energy and Clinton Global initiatives in developing baseline, financial and education programs.

PROJECT X CONSTRUCTION, INC. *(Atlanta, GA)* .... 2008 – 2015

PROJECT X CONSTRUCTION, INC. *(Atlanta, GA)* .... 2008 – 2015
A startup general construction company in the retail banking, restaurant and tenant improvement market with 25 staff members.

PRESIDENT / OWNER
Founded and grew company from start-up, providing sales, preconstruction, estimation and over-flow project management. Achieved and maintained general contracting licenses in TN, GA, NC, VA and SC.

Key Achievements:
- Created a consistent execution platform through the implementation of company intranet, providing templates for 18 project stages and details of project processes, responsibilities and accountabilities.

- Established and managed the Atlanta Office, driving company growth from $10M to $35M per year by developing strategic clients such as Chick-Fil-A, JP Morgan Chase and Kroger.

FACILITY GROUP *(Atlanta, GA)* .... 2004 – 2008
A $450M global full-service planning, design and program management firm in industrial and public markets with 400 staff members.

EXECUTIVE VICE PRESIDENT / CHIEF OPERATING OFFICER
Managed worldwide construction operations in three US offices, Europe and South Pacific.

Key Achievements:
- Generated more than $300M in new business by creating effective sales presentations.

- Led the strategic reorganization of the entire construction company through establishment of project engineering for market segment managers, defining internal process and performance goals.

- Developed a new safety program, providing focus on education, support and personal responsibility, resulting in achieving no lost time accidents recorded.

CENTEX CONSTRUCTION GROUP *(Atlanta, GA)* .... 2001 – 2004
A large $2B year commercial construction division of Centex Homes, a publically traded residential developer.

VICE PRESIDENT, EDUCATION UNIT
Created a new geographic division in Georgia, providing a focus on qualification-based selections in K-12, higher, and technical education markets. Managed business unit sales of $200M with the Technical College System of Georgia, Fulton County Schools, DeKalb County Schools, Atlanta Public Schools, and Georgia State Finance and Investment Commission.

Key Achievements:
- Improved overall project performance by creating new operations procedures.

Education

BACHELOR OF SCIENCE, INDUSTRIAL CONSTRUCTION MANAGEMENT
COLORADO STATE UNIVERSITY, FORT COLLINS, CO

Community Involvement

International knowledge and research center for green building, Southern Polytechnic State University, 2010-present

Former:
Cobb county heart ball, American heart association, chairman 2015
Marietta Redevelopment Coordinator, Director

More Tips

Action Verbs

The following pages consist of words that you may find useful to show action when describing your duties or accomplishments on a resume. There may be some you hear of quite often that are not on the list. This is because I try to stay away from the most commonly used, clichéd or older sounding verbs. Take a look and try them out!

Wendy's Favorite Action Verbs for Résumés

Abated	Bounded	Contracted	Drive	Formalized
Abide	Braced	Contributed	Drove	Formulated
Abounded	Branched	Controlled	Earned	Fortified
Absorbed	Braved	Converged	Eclipsed	Forwarded
Accelerated	Breathed	Conveyed	Edited	Fostered
Accepted	Bred	Convinced	Educated	Founded
Acclaimed	Brief	Coordinated	Elaborated	Frequented
Acclimated	Briefed	Countered	Elected	Fueled
Accommodated	Brightened	Created	Elevated	Functioned
Accomplished	Bristled	Cultivated	Elicited	Funneled
Accounted	Broached	Declared	Eliminated	Furnished
Accrued	Broadcasted	Decorated	Embarked	Furthered
Accumulated	Broadened	Decreased	Embedded	Fused
Achieved	Brought	Dedicated	Embraced	Gained
Acknowledged	Budgeted	Defeated	Emerged	Galvanized
Acted	Buffered	Defended	Emitted	Gathered
Activated	Built	Defined	Employed	Gauged
Actuated	Bypassed	Deflated	Empowered	Geared
Adapted	Calculated	Delegated	Emulated	Generated
Addressed	Calmed	Deliver	Enabled	Gesticulated
Adhered	Campaigned	Delivered	Enacted	Governed
Adjoined	Captured	Demonstrated	Encouraged	Graced
Adjourned	Catapulted	Deployed	Enforced	Graded
Adjusted	Ceased	Designated	Enhanced	Graduated
Administered	Cemented	Designed	Enlightened	Granted
Admitted	Centralized	Detailed	Enlivened	Greeted
Advanced	Certified	Detected	Entertained	Groomed
Advised	Certified	Determined	Enticed	Grouped
Advocated	Challenged	Deterred	Entrusted	Guard
Affirmed	Championed	Detracted	Envisioned	Guarded
Alerted	Channeled	Developed	Escalated	Guide
Alleviated	Charted	Deviated	Established	Guided
Allied	Choreographed	Devised	Evolved	Hailed
Amended	Circulated	Devoted	Excelled	Halted
Analyzed	Classified	Diagnosed	Executed	Handled
Applied	Clenched	Differentiated	Exerted	Harbored
Apprehended	Closed	Diminished	Exorcised	Hauled
Appropriated	Coached	Diminished	Exposed	Head
Assigned	Collaborated	Disarmed	Expressed	Headed
Assisted	Collected	Discerned	Extracted	Heightened
Augmented	Combined	Disclosed	Exuded	Held
Balanced	Commended	Discounted	Facilitated	Helped
Beautified	Committed	Dispatch	Fashioned	Highlighted
Beautified	Compiled	Dispatched	Flourished	Hired
Blazed	Comprised	Disseminated	Focused	Hoisted
Blocked	Condensed	Dissolved	Foiled	Honored
Boasted	Conducted	Dissuaded	Forecast	Housed
Booked	Connected	Distinguished	Forecasted	Hunted
Boosted	Conquered	Diverted	Foresaw	Hydrated
Bought	Consulted	Dominated	Forked	Identified

Wendy's Favorite Action Verbs for Résumés

Identify	Linked	Partnered	Quoted	Resolved
Ignited	Loaded	Patrolled	Raised	Resorted
Illuminated	Localized	Penetrated	Rationalized	Respond
Illustrated	Located	Perfected	Reached	Responded
Immersed	Locked	Performed	Reacquainted	Restarted
Impacted	Logged	Personalized	Reactivated	Restored
Imparted	Magnetized	Personified	Readjusted	Restructured
Implemented	Maintained	Piloted	Realigned	Resumed
Implored	Manage	Pioneered	Reaped	Resumed
Impressed	Managed	Placated	Rearranged	Resurrected
Improved	Mandated	Polarized	Reasoned	Resuscitated
Included	Maneuvered	Polled	Reasserted	Retained
Incorporated	Manned	Portrayed	Reassured	Retreated
Increased	Manufactured	Positioned	Rebounded	Revamped
Inferred	Mapped	Postulated	Rebuilt	Revitalized
Influenced	Market	Practiced	Recaptured	Revived
Informed	Marketed	Praised	Received	Rose
Initiated	Mastered	Predicted	Reclaimed	Rotated
Inspired	Masterminded	Prepackaged	Recognized	Salvaged
Installed	Matched	Prepared	Recommend	Satisfied
Instituted	Materialized	Prescribed	Recommended	Saturated
Instructed	Matriculated	Preserved	Reconciled	Saved
Integrated	Maximized	Presided	Reconditioned	Scouted
Intervened	Mended	Presumed	Reconstructed	Screened
Interviewed	Merged	Prevailed	Reconvened	Scrubbed
Introduced	Migrated	Prevented	Recouped	Sculpted
Investigated	Mitigated	Proclaimed	Recovered	Sealed
Invigorated	Monitored	Procured	Recruited	Seceded
Isolated	Motivated	Progressed	Reduced	Secured
Issued	Navigated	Projected	Reemerged	Seized
Itemize	Negotiated	Proliferated	Reestablished	Selected
Itemized	Netted	Promoted	Refashioned	Separated
Jelled	Nominated	Prompted	Reformed	Serve
Joined	Normalized	Promulgated	Reformulated	Served
Jotted	Notified	Propelled	Refreshed	Serviced
Journeyed	Nurtured	Proposed	Regained	Shaped
Justified	Observed	Proposition	Registered	Simplified
Jutted	Obtained	Prosecuted	Reinforced	Slashed
Kept	Officiated	Protected	Rejoined	Soared
Keynoted	Optimized	Proved	Remained	Sold
Kick-started	Orchestrated	Provided	Remodeled	Solicited
Labored	Organized	Publicized	Rendered	Solidified
Laid	Originated	Published	Renewed	Spearhead
Launched	Outlined	Purchased	Repaired	Spearheaded
Lead	Outsourced	Purged	Replaced	Specified
Leaped	Outweighed	Quadrupled	Replenished	Spruced
Lecture	Overhauled	Qualified	Reported	Spurred
Lectured	Own	Quantified	Repositioned	Stabilized
Led	Packaged	Queried	Reproduced	Standardized
Leveraged	Participated	Quizzed	Requested	Steer

Wendy's Favorite Action Verbs for Résumés

Steered	Used
Stimulated	Ushered
Stirred	Utilized
Streamlined	Validated
Strengthened	Veered
Stretched	Ventured
Structured	Vied
Studied	Viewed
Styled	Visited
Submitted	Visualized
Subscribed	Vocalized
Succeeded	Volunteer
Suggested	Volunteered
Summarized	Voted
Supervise	Xeroxed
Supervised	Yielded
Supplemented	Zapped
Supplied	Zeroed
Supported	Zoned
Surged	
Surpassed	
Sustained	
Swept	
Switched	
Synchronized	
Taught	
Terminated	
Thrived	
Traced	
Tracked	
Transcended	
Transformed	
Translated	
Transmitted	
Transported	
Traveled	
Treated	
Triggered	
Tripled	
Triumphed	
Truncated	
Uncovered	
Undertook	
Unified	
United	
Unscrambled	
Updated	
Upgraded	
Uprooted	
Urged	

INDEX

About the Author

Wendy Steele started occasionally writing and critiquing resumes for colleagues in corporate America in the early '90s. Her coworkers nominated her "Most Studious" and actually presented her with an award. She never thought she would write resumes for a living, and if you've read her Good Housekeeping article: "My Brilliant New Career,"

 https://www.goodhousekeeping.com/life/career/advice/a12417/career-change-advice/

you'll see that she didn't know such companies even existed. After being laid off from her IT job of nearly 12 years, and putting her literary career on hold, she switched her pen to writing resumes, founded BluePrint Resumes & Consulting, and quickly grew her full service firm to multiple locations throughout the U.S.

Wendy is a Certified Professional Resume Writer, as well as a Career and Job Search Consultant. BluePrint Resumes & Consulting is the only company of its kind with a global client base. Check out her first nonfiction title: Let Me Get My Coffee! Then We'll Talk Business, a memoir/self-help book about how she started and grew the company.

Several Fortune 500 companies call Wendy and her team to lead workshops or to write resumes for their employees whenever they're downsizing or restructuring. This includes the Marriott, Pepsico, Doral Bank, and many others. She has led presentations at Clark Atlanta University, McKesson, various churches and also assisted Women-for-Hire in conducting resume critiques for job seekers.

Wendy is a proud member of the Professional Association of Resume Writers and Career Coaches, and the National Resume Writers Association. BluePrint Resumes and Consulting has been featured in the Atlanta Journal Constitution, on the Best 10 Resumes site, and highly reputable review sites. You can also find her work in "Modernize Your Job Search Letters" by Wendy Enelow and Louise Kursmark. She has a strong senior-level client base, and assists C-level executives of some of the most recognized brands. Since she is considered "a life saver" by many for her expertise in writing resumes for numerous industries, Wendy is recommended by many executive recruiters throughout the U.S. She regularly attends career industry conferences, has certifications in business and career coaching, and stays abreast of the industry to help job seekers put their best foot forward and achieve the career of their dreams.

For more information about Wendy or BluePrint Resumes & Consulting, visit **www.wendydsteele.com or www.blueprintresumes.com**

Made in the USA
Coppell, TX
05 November 2021

65237310R00118